nickelodeon™

降 击 神 通

THE LAST AIRBENDER™

Created by
Bryan Konietzko
Michael Dante DiMartino

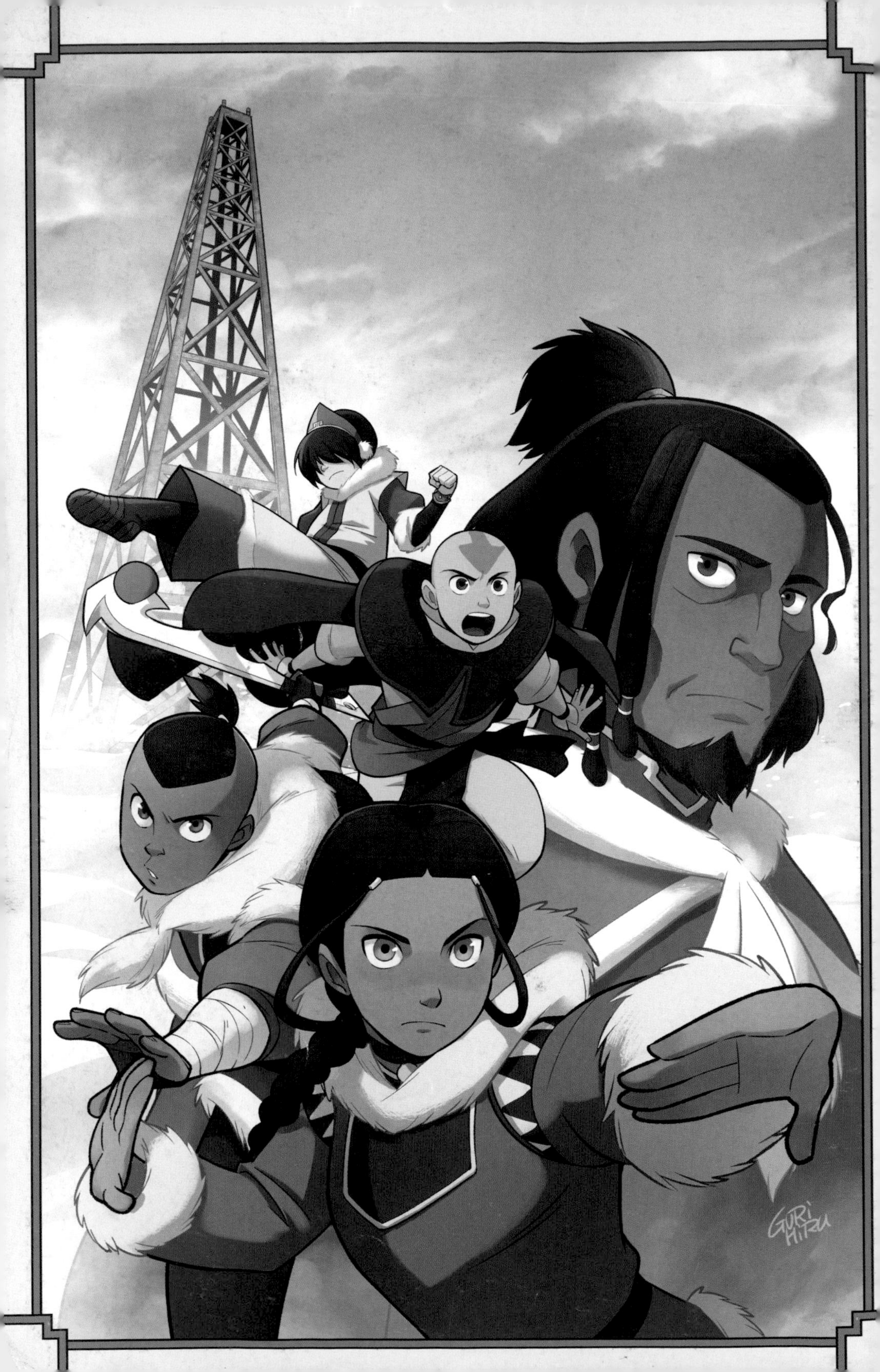
GURI HIRU

nickelodeon™

降击神通

AVATAR

THE LAST AIRBENDER™

NORTH AND SOUTH · PART TWO

script
GENE LUEN YANG

art and cover
GURIHIRU

lettering
MICHAEL HEISLER

DARK HORSE BOOKS

president and publisher
MIKE RICHARDSON

editor
DAVE MARSHALL

assistant editor
RACHEL ROBERTS

collection designer
SARAH TERRY

digital art technician
CHRISTIANNE GOUDREAU

Special thanks to Linda Lee, Kat van Dam, James Salerno, and Joan Hilty
at Nickelodeon, and to Bryan Konietzko and Michael Dante DiMartino.

Published by **Dark Horse Books**
A division of Dark Horse Comics, Inc.
10956 SE Main Street, Milwaukie, OR 97222

DarkHorse.com
Nick.com

International Licensing: (503) 905-2377
Comic Shop Locator Service: (888) 266-4226

First edition: January 2017 | ISBN 978-1-50670-129-5

1 3 5 7 9 10 8 6 4 2
Printed in China

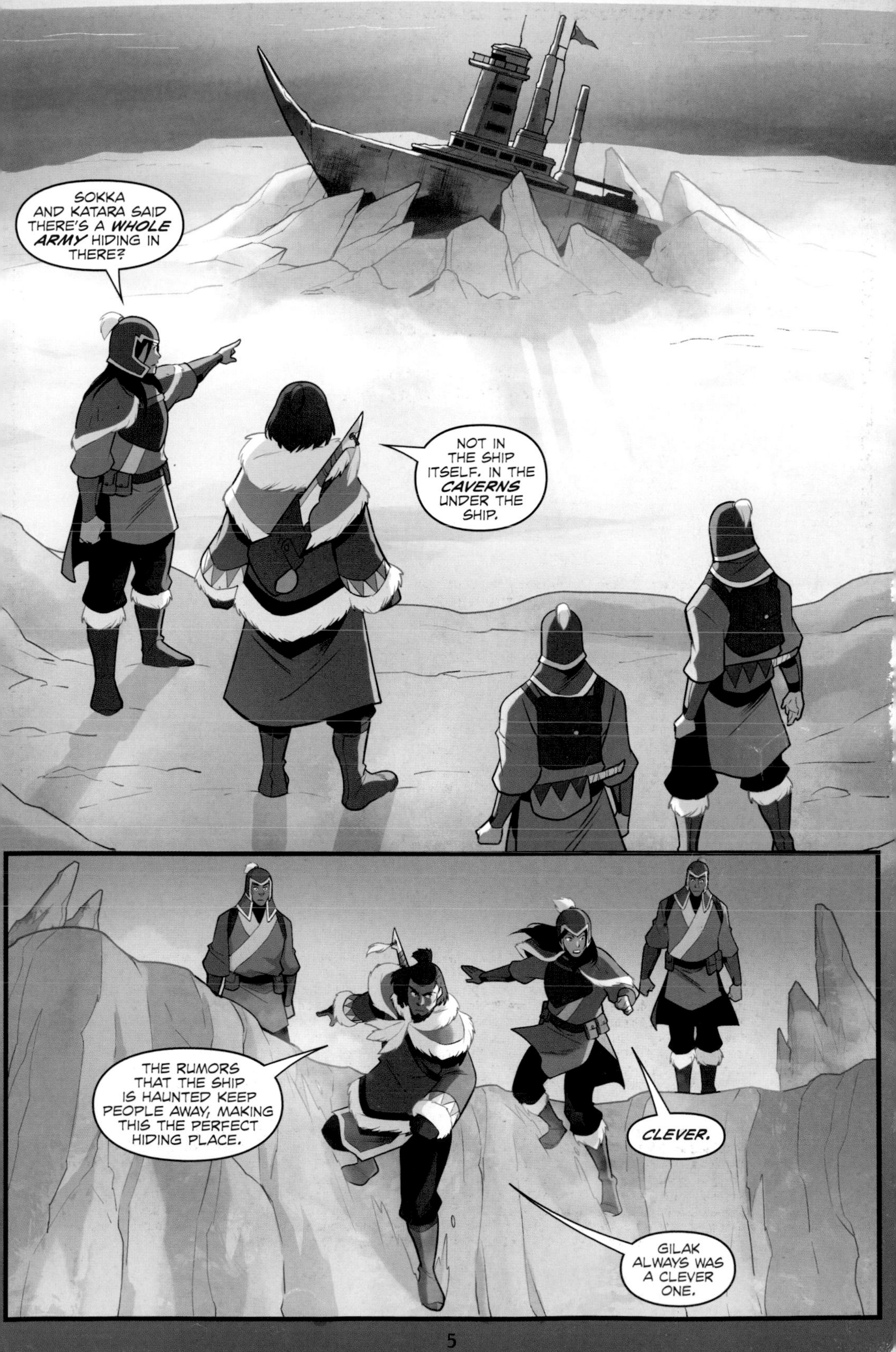
SOKKA AND KATARA SAID THERE'S A *WHOLE ARMY* HIDING IN THERE?
NOT IN THE SHIP ITSELF. IN THE *CAVERNS* UNDER THE SHIP.
THE RUMORS THAT THE SHIP IS HAUNTED KEEP PEOPLE AWAY, MAKING THIS THE PERFECT HIDING PLACE.
CLEVER.
GILAK ALWAYS WAS A CLEVER ONE.

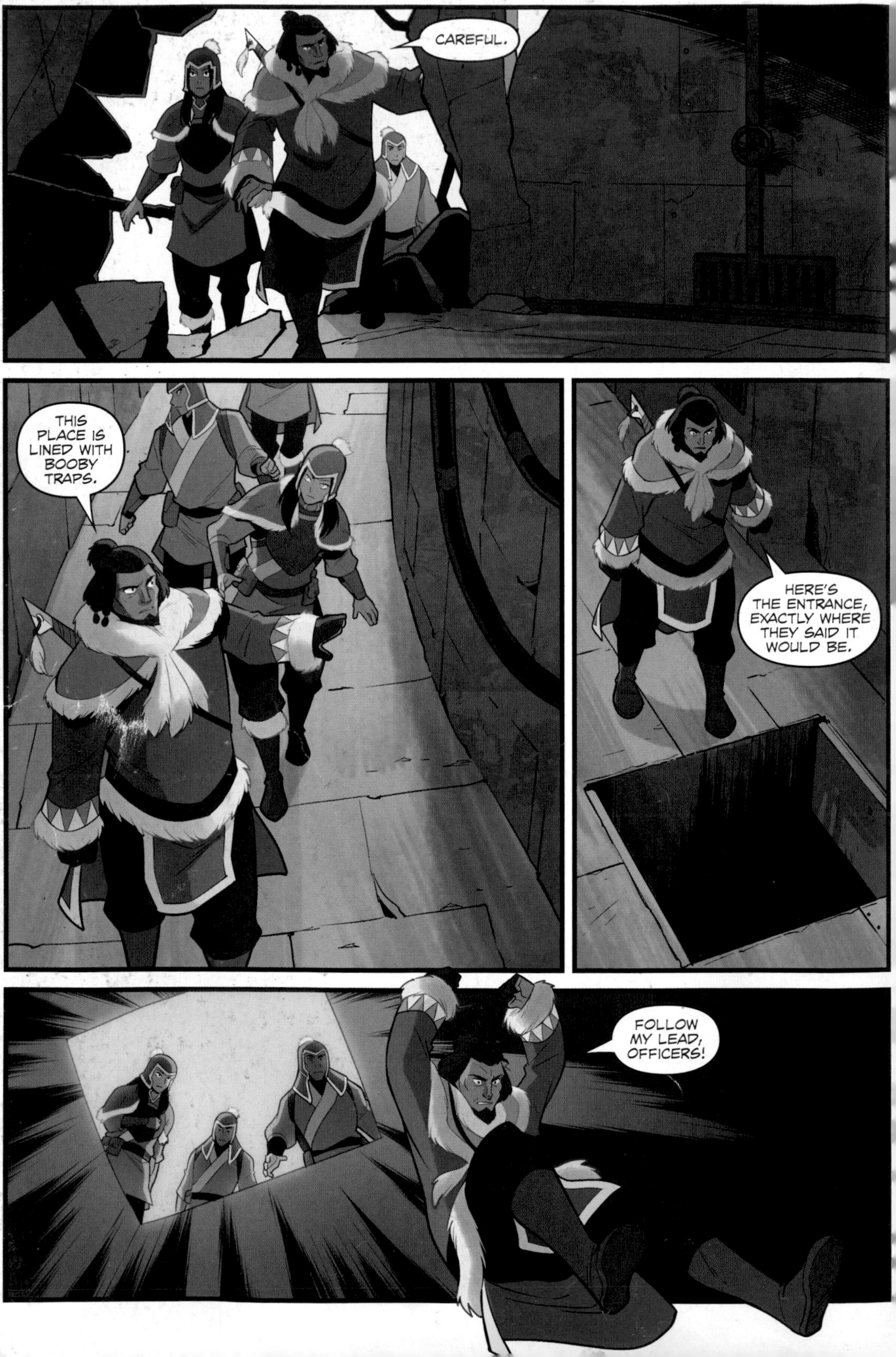
CAREFUL.
THIS PLACE IS LINED WITH BOOBY TRAPS.
HERE'S THE ENTRANCE, EXACTLY WHERE THEY SAID IT WOULD BE.
FOLLOW MY LEAD, OFFICERS!

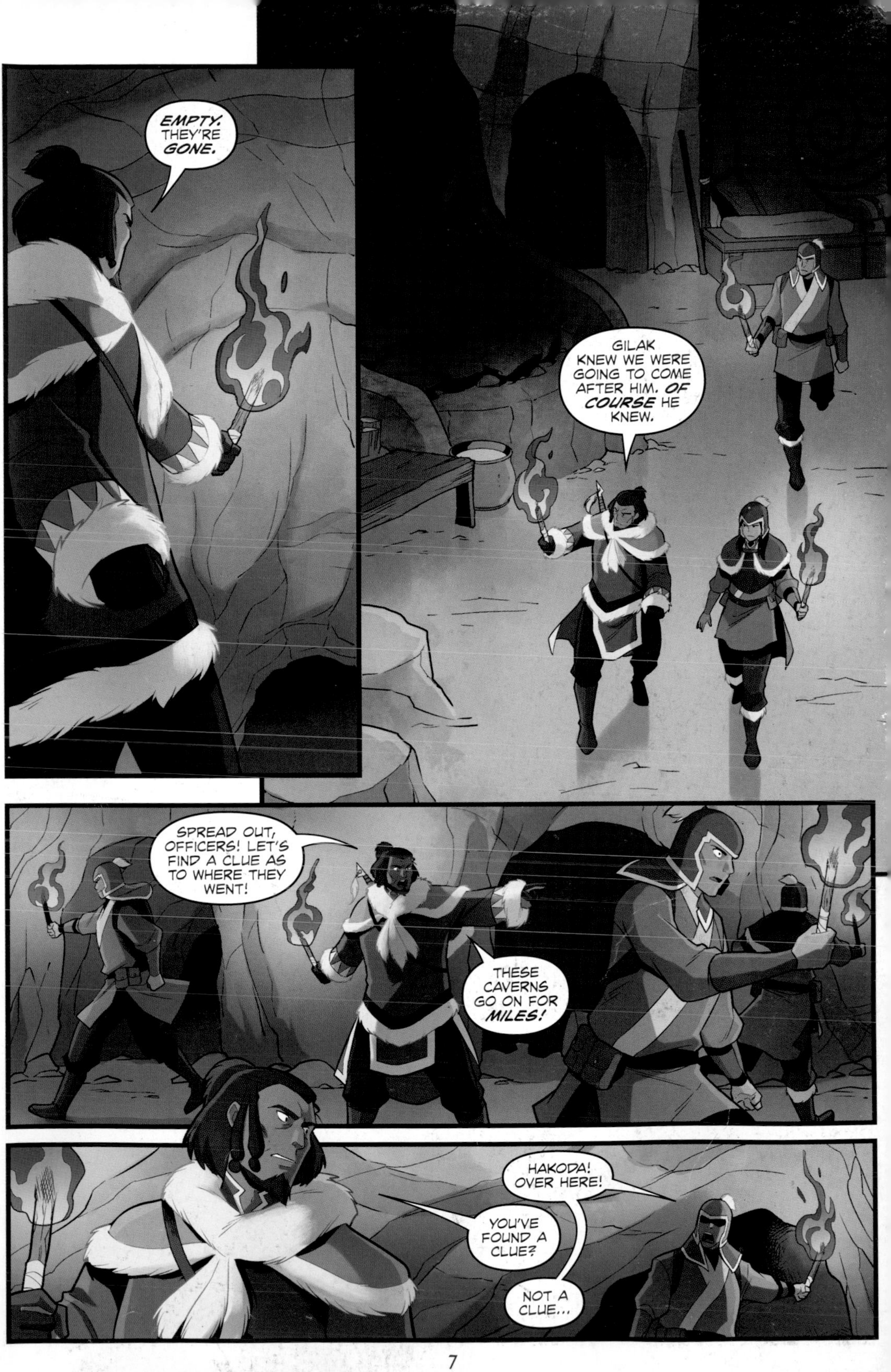
EMPTY. THEY'RE GONE.
GILAK KNEW WE WERE GOING TO COME AFTER HIM. OF COURSE HE KNEW.
SPREAD OUT, OFFICERS! LET'S FIND A CLUE AS TO WHERE THEY WENT!
THESE CAVERNS GO ON FOR MILES!
HAKODA! OVER HERE!
YOU'VE FOUND A CLUE?
NOT A CLUE...

酋長
吾不久將受於真相
A MESSAGE.
TRANSLATION:
SOON I WILL SHOW YOU THE TRUTH, CHIEFTAIN.

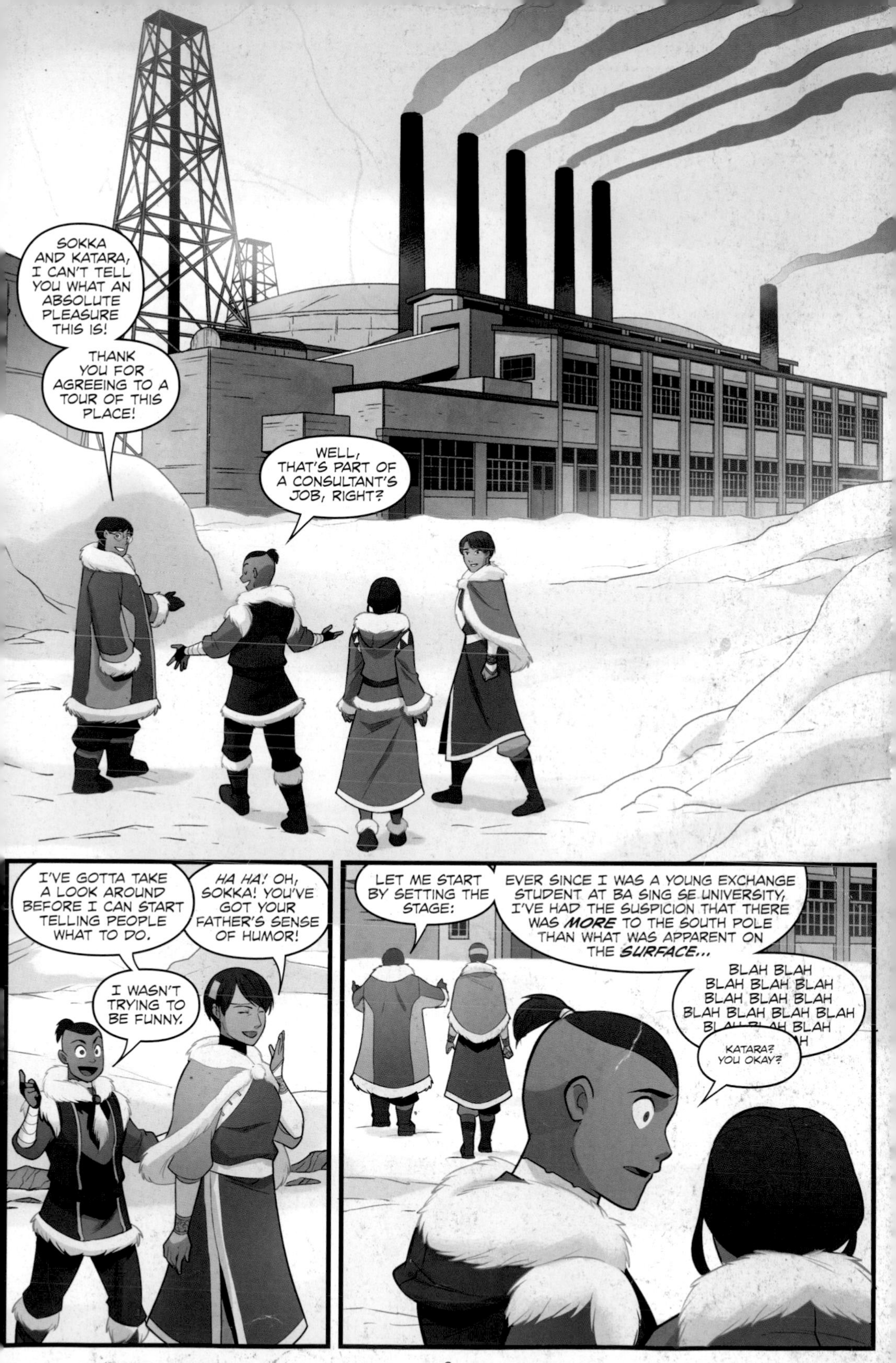
SOKKA AND KATARA, I CAN'T TELL YOU WHAT AN ABSOLUTE PLEASURE THIS IS!
THANK YOU FOR AGREEING TO A TOUR OF THIS PLACE!
WELL, THAT'S PART OF A CONSULTANT'S JOB, RIGHT?
I'VE GOTTA TAKE A LOOK AROUND BEFORE I CAN START TELLING PEOPLE WHAT TO DO.
HA HA! OH, SOKKA! YOU'VE GOT YOUR FATHER'S SENSE OF HUMOR!
I WASN'T TRYING TO BE FUNNY.
LET ME START BY SETTING THE STAGE:
EVER SINCE I WAS A YOUNG EXCHANGE STUDENT AT BA SING SE UNIVERSITY, I'VE HAD THE SUSPICION THAT THERE WAS MORE TO THE SOUTH POLE THAN WHAT WAS APPARENT ON THE SURFACE...
BLAH BLAH BLAH BLAH BLAH BLAH BLAH BLAH BLAH BLAH BLAH BLAH BLAH
KATARA? YOU OKAY?

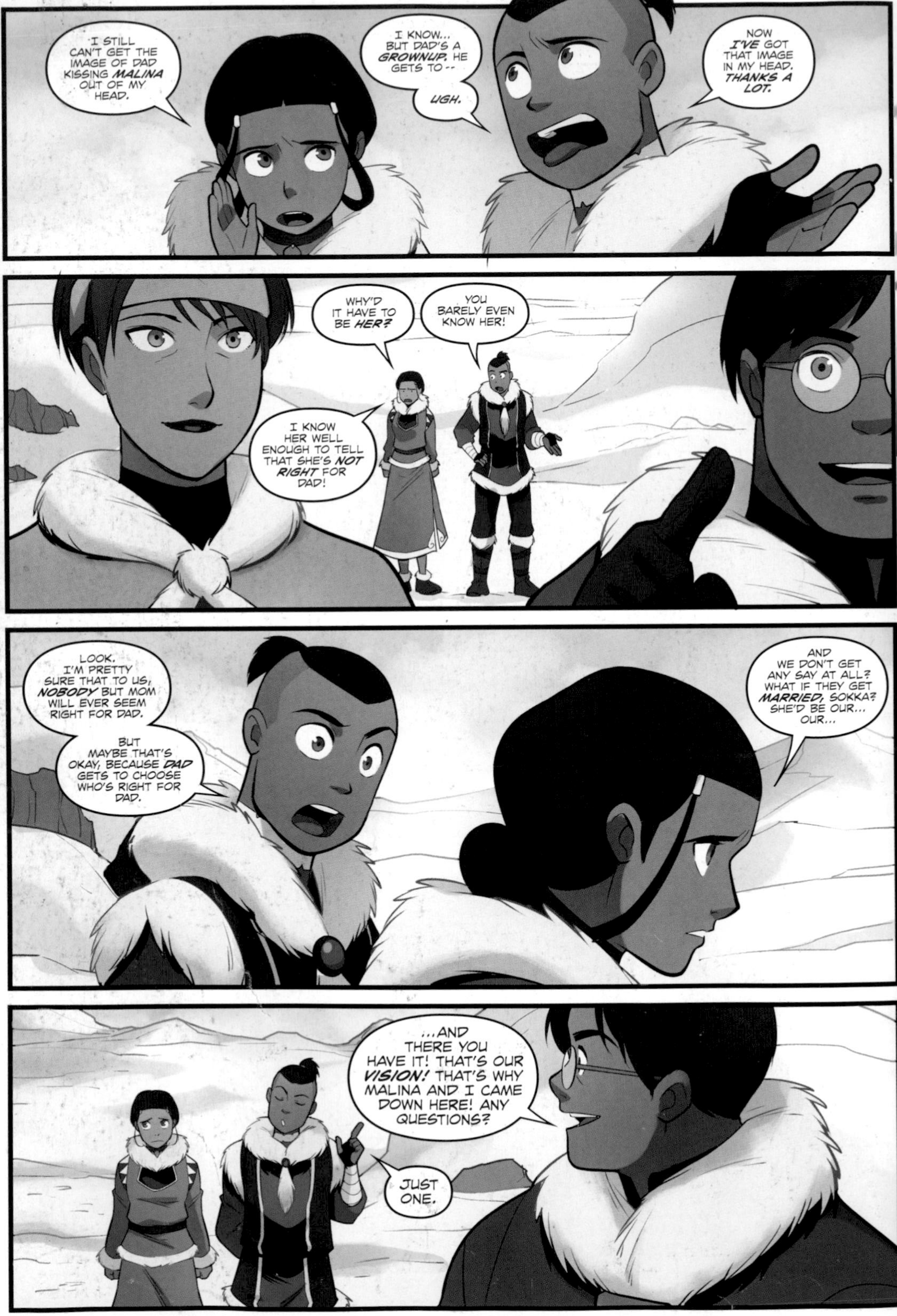
I STILL CAN'T GET THE IMAGE OF DAD KISSING MALINA OUT OF MY HEAD.
I KNOW... BUT DAD'S A GROWNUP. HE GETS TO--
UGH.
NOW I'VE GOT THAT IMAGE IN MY HEAD. THANKS A LOT.
WHY'D IT HAVE TO BE HER?
YOU BARELY EVEN KNOW HER!
I KNOW HER WELL ENOUGH TO TELL THAT SHE'S NOT RIGHT FOR DAD!
LOOK. I'M PRETTY SURE THAT TO US, NOBODY BUT MOM WILL EVER SEEM RIGHT FOR DAD.
BUT MAYBE THAT'S OKAY, BECAUSE DAD GETS TO CHOOSE WHO'S RIGHT FOR DAD.
AND WE DON'T GET ANY SAY AT ALL? WHAT IF THEY GET MARRIED, SOKKA? SHE'D BE OUR... OUR...
...AND THERE YOU HAVE IT! THAT'S OUR VISION! THAT'S WHY MALINA AND I CAME DOWN HERE! ANY QUESTIONS?
JUST ONE.

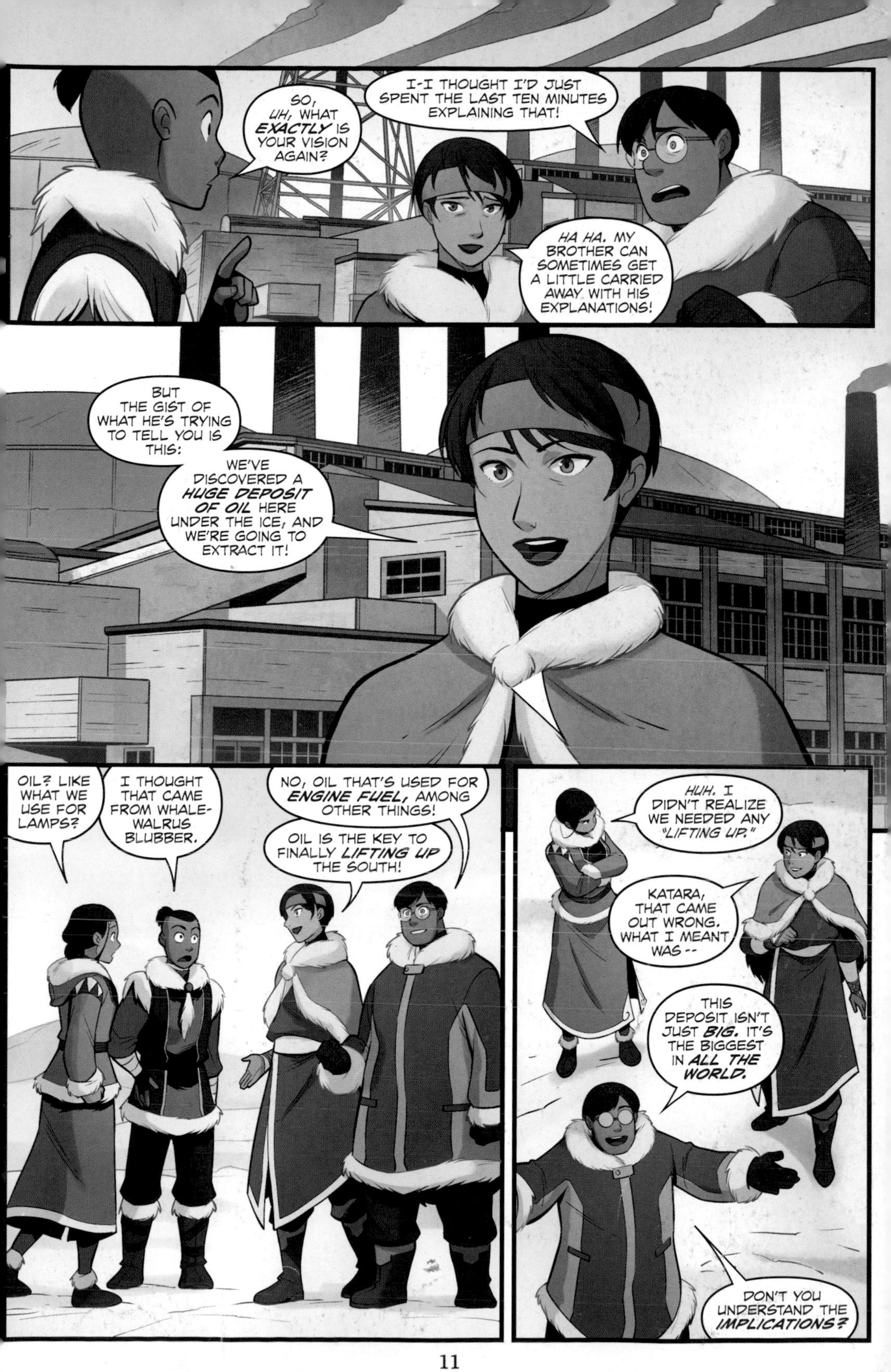
SO, UH, WHAT EXACTLY IS YOUR VISION AGAIN?
I-I THOUGHT I'D JUST SPENT THE LAST TEN MINUTES EXPLAINING THAT!
HA HA. MY BROTHER CAN SOMETIMES GET A LITTLE CARRIED AWAY WITH HIS EXPLANATIONS!
BUT THE GIST OF WHAT HE'S TRYING TO TELL YOU IS THIS:
WE'VE DISCOVERED A HUGE DEPOSIT OF OIL HERE UNDER THE ICE, AND WE'RE GOING TO EXTRACT IT!
OIL? LIKE WHAT WE USE FOR LAMPS?
I THOUGHT THAT CAME FROM WHALE-WALRUS BLUBBER.
NO, OIL THAT'S USED FOR ENGINE FUEL, AMONG OTHER THINGS!
OIL IS THE KEY TO FINALLY LIFTING UP THE SOUTH!
HUH. I DIDN'T REALIZE WE NEEDED ANY "LIFTING UP."
KATARA, THAT CAME OUT WRONG. WHAT I MEANT WAS --
THIS DEPOSIT ISN'T JUST BIG. IT'S THE BIGGEST IN ALL THE WORLD.
DON'T YOU UNDERSTAND THE IMPLICATIONS?

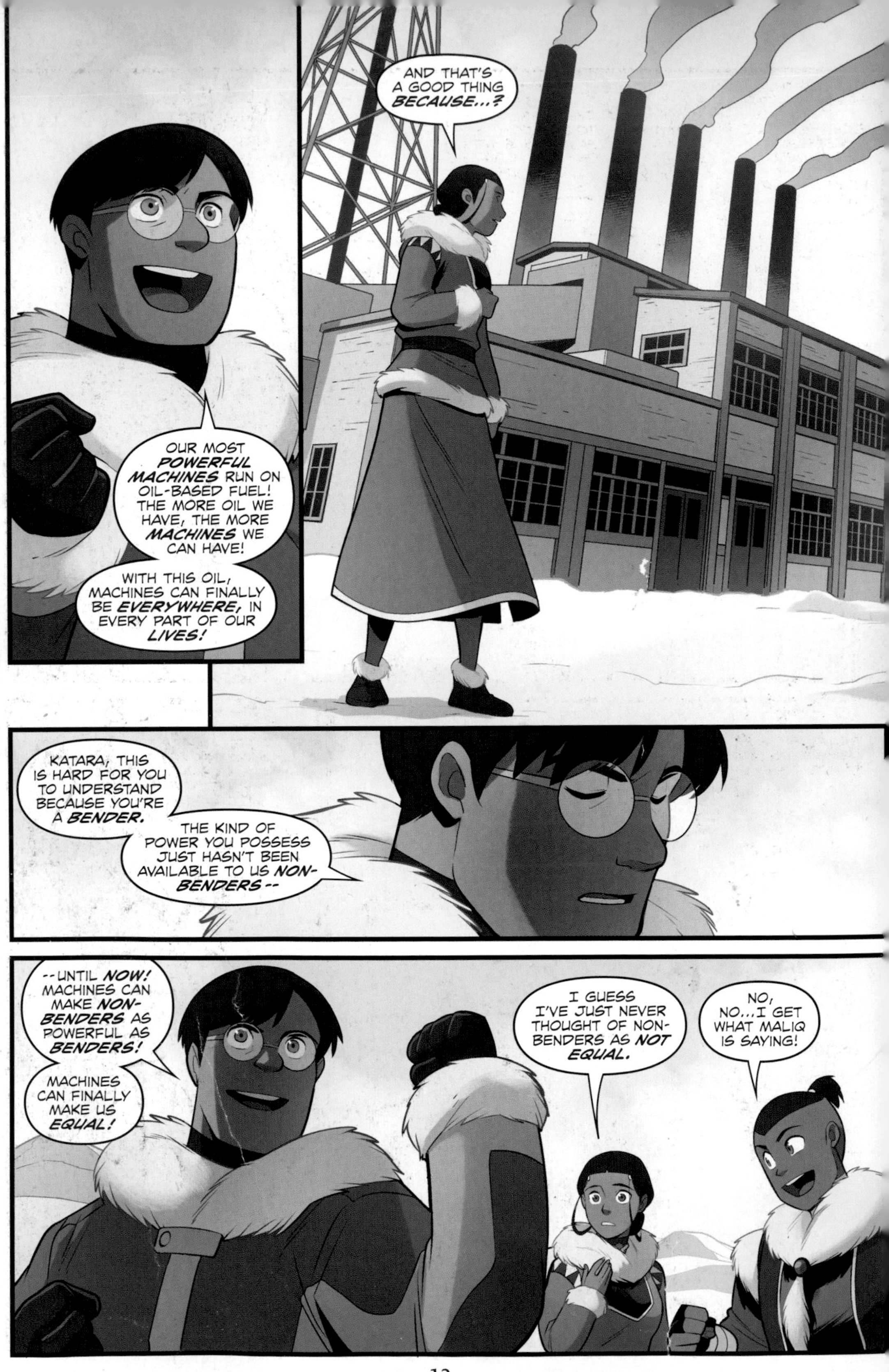
AND THAT'S A GOOD THING BECAUSE...?
OUR MOST POWERFUL MACHINES RUN ON OIL-BASED FUEL! THE MORE OIL WE HAVE, THE MORE MACHINES WE CAN HAVE!
WITH THIS OIL, MACHINES CAN FINALLY BE EVERYWHERE, IN EVERY PART OF OUR LIVES!
KATARA, THIS IS HARD FOR YOU TO UNDERSTAND BECAUSE YOU'RE A BENDER.
THE KIND OF POWER YOU POSSESS JUST HASN'T BEEN AVAILABLE TO US NON-BENDERS --
--UNTIL NOW! MACHINES CAN MAKE NON-BENDERS AS POWERFUL AS BENDERS!
MACHINES CAN FINALLY MAKE US EQUAL!
I GUESS I'VE JUST NEVER THOUGHT OF NON-BENDERS AS NOT EQUAL.
NO, NO...I GET WHAT MALIQ IS SAYING!

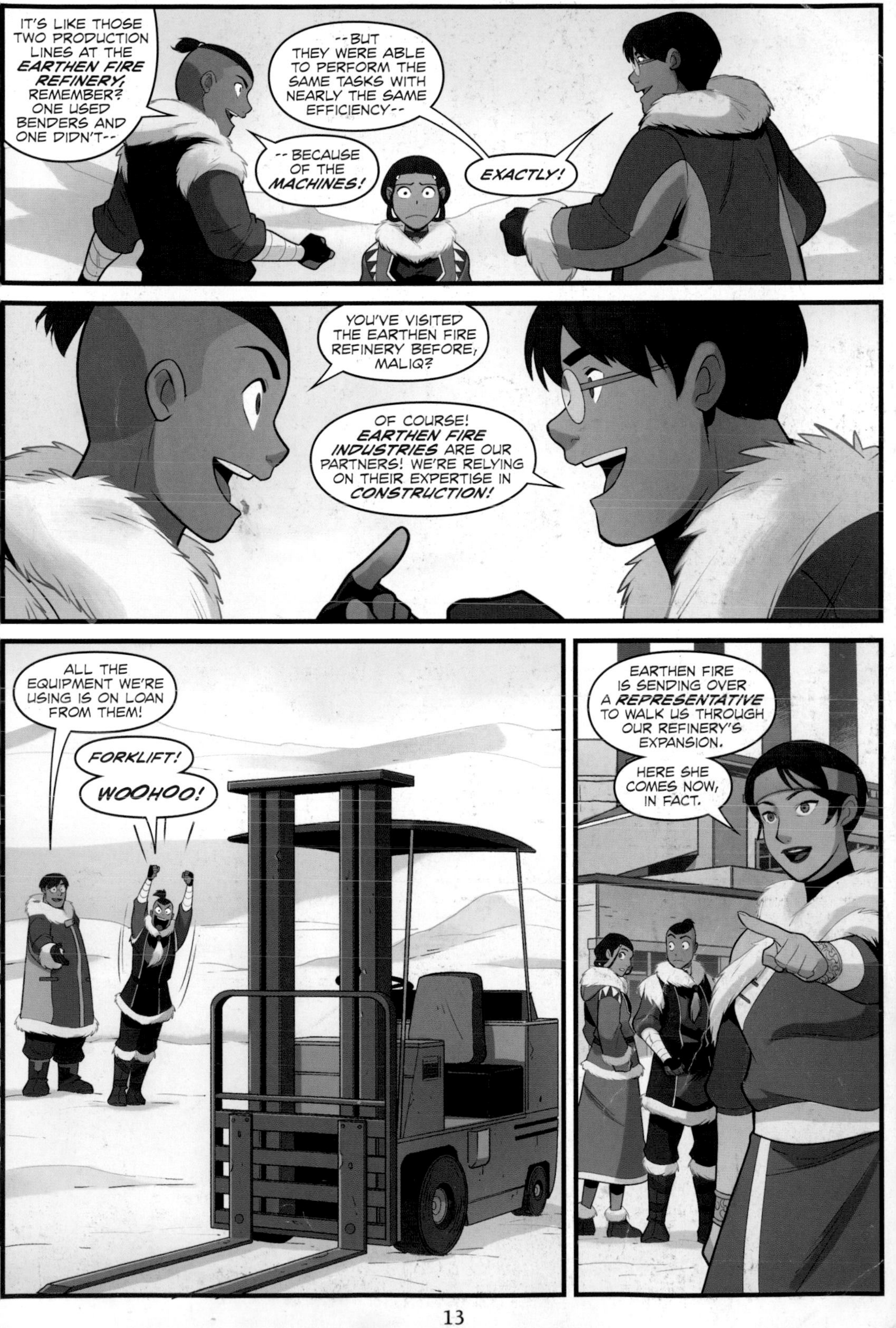
IT'S LIKE THOSE TWO PRODUCTION LINES AT THE EARTHEN FIRE REFINERY, REMEMBER? ONE USED BENDERS AND ONE DIDN'T--
--BUT THEY WERE ABLE TO PERFORM THE SAME TASKS WITH NEARLY THE SAME EFFICIENCY--
--BECAUSE OF THE MACHINES!
EXACTLY!
YOU'VE VISITED THE EARTHEN FIRE REFINERY BEFORE, MALIQ?
OF COURSE! EARTHEN FIRE INDUSTRIES ARE OUR PARTNERS! WE'RE RELYING ON THEIR EXPERTISE IN CONSTRUCTION!
ALL THE EQUIPMENT WE'RE USING IS ON LOAN FROM THEM!
FORKLIFT!
WOOHOO!
EARTHEN FIRE IS SENDING OVER A REPRESENTATIVE TO WALK US THROUGH OUR REFINERY'S EXPANSION.
HERE SHE COMES NOW, IN FACT.

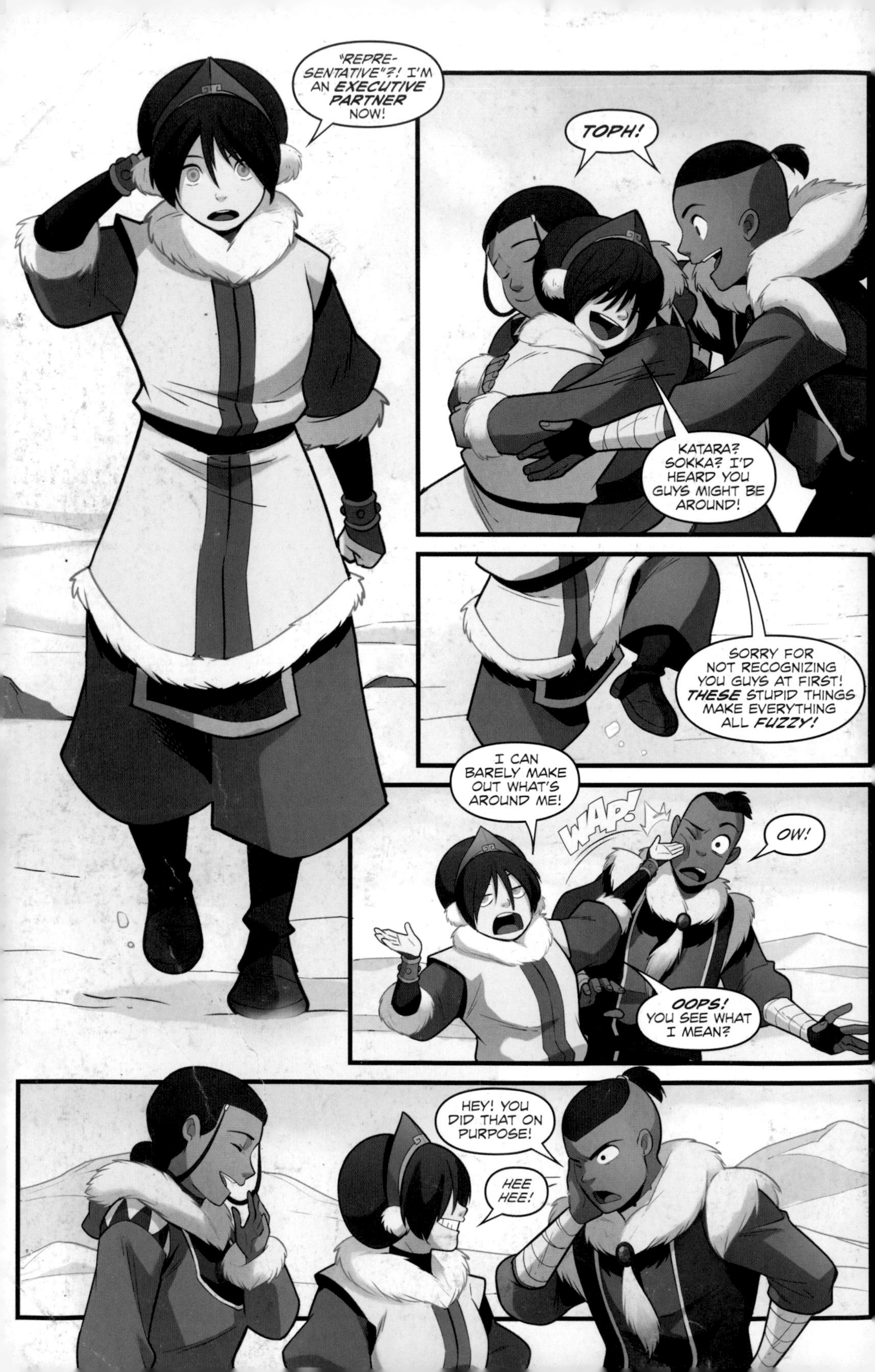
"REPRE-SENTATIVE"?! I'M AN EXECUTIVE PARTNER NOW!
TOPH!
KATARA? SOKKA? I'D HEARD YOU GUYS MIGHT BE AROUND!
SORRY FOR NOT RECOGNIZING YOU GUYS AT FIRST! THESE STUPID THINGS MAKE EVERYTHING ALL FUZZY!
I CAN BARELY MAKE OUT WHAT'S AROUND ME!
WAP!
OW!
OOPS! YOU SEE WHAT I MEAN?
HEY! YOU DID THAT ON PURPOSE!
HEE HEE!

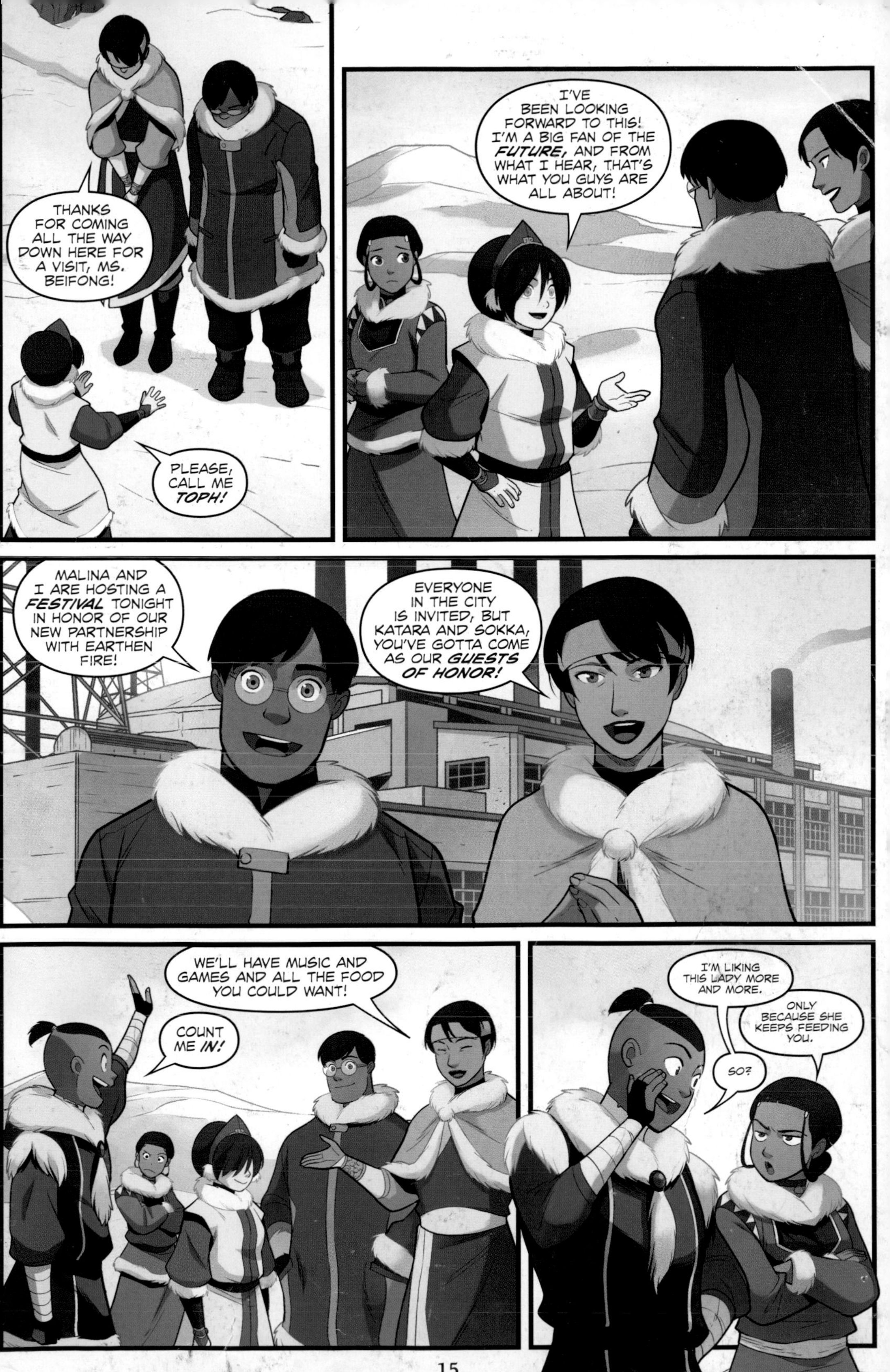
THANKS FOR COMING ALL THE WAY DOWN HERE FOR A VISIT, MS. BEIFONG!
PLEASE, CALL ME TOPH!
I'VE BEEN LOOKING FORWARD TO THIS! I'M A BIG FAN OF THE FUTURE, AND FROM WHAT I HEAR, THAT'S WHAT YOU GUYS ARE ALL ABOUT!
MALINA AND I ARE HOSTING A FESTIVAL TONIGHT IN HONOR OF OUR NEW PARTNERSHIP WITH EARTHEN FIRE!
EVERYONE IN THE CITY IS INVITED, BUT KATARA AND SOKKA, YOU'VE GOTTA COME AS OUR GUESTS OF HONOR!
WE'LL HAVE MUSIC AND GAMES AND ALL THE FOOD YOU COULD WANT!
COUNT ME IN!
I'M LIKING THIS LADY MORE AND MORE.
ONLY BECAUSE SHE KEEPS FEEDING YOU.
SO?

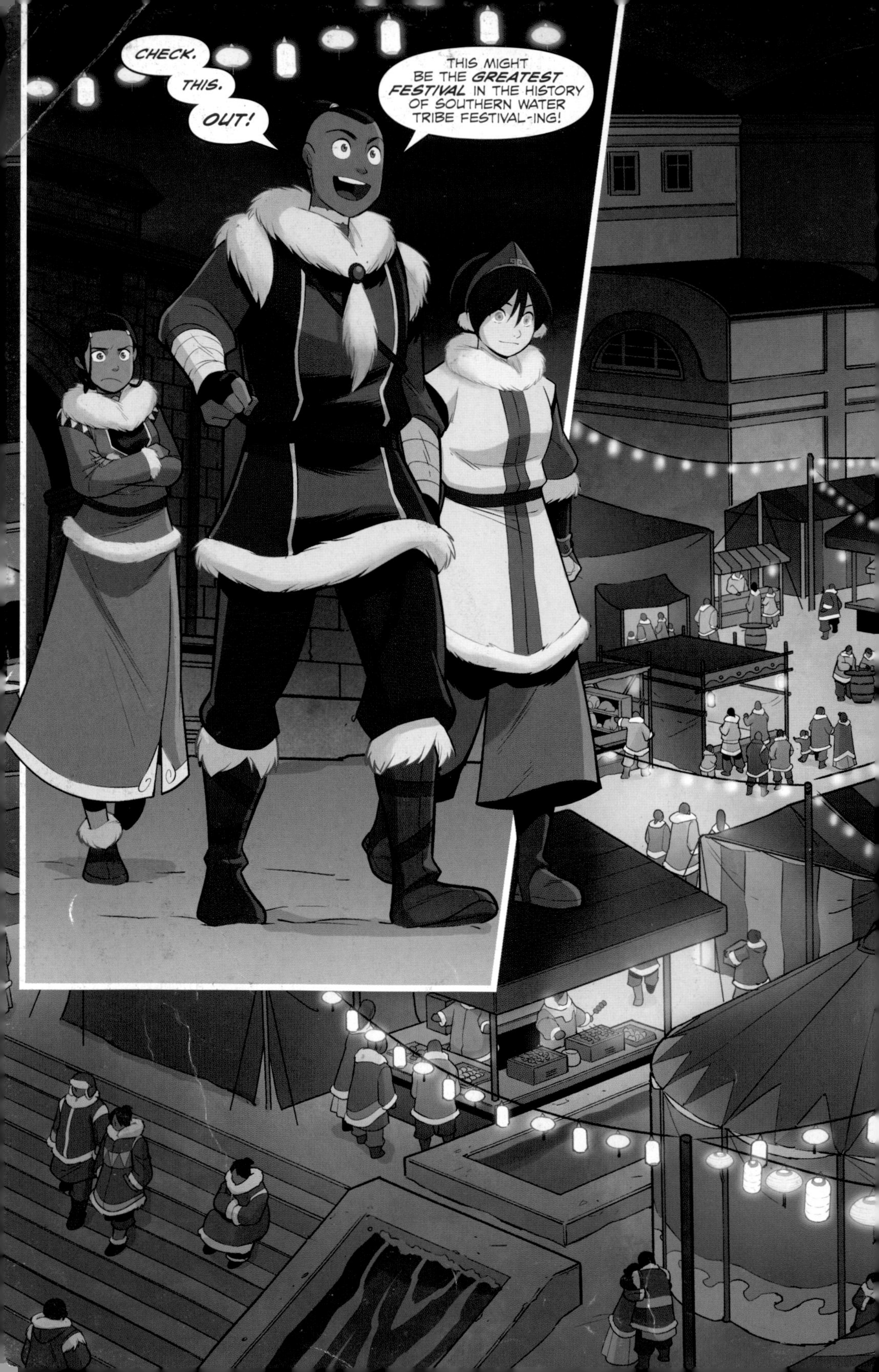
CHECK.
THIS.
OUT!
THIS MIGHT BE THE GREATEST FESTIVAL IN THE HISTORY OF SOUTHERN WATER TRIBE FESTIVAL-ING!

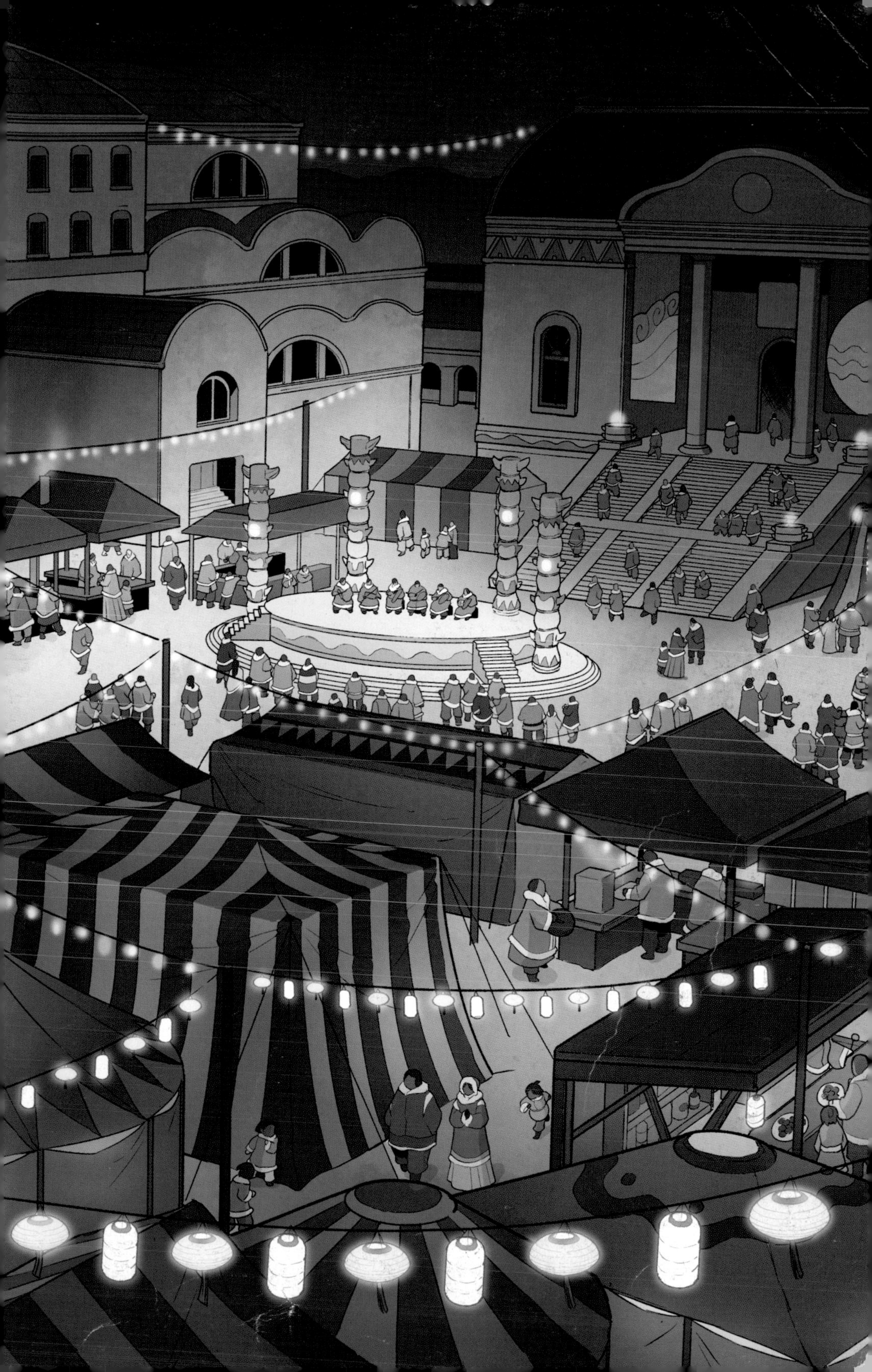

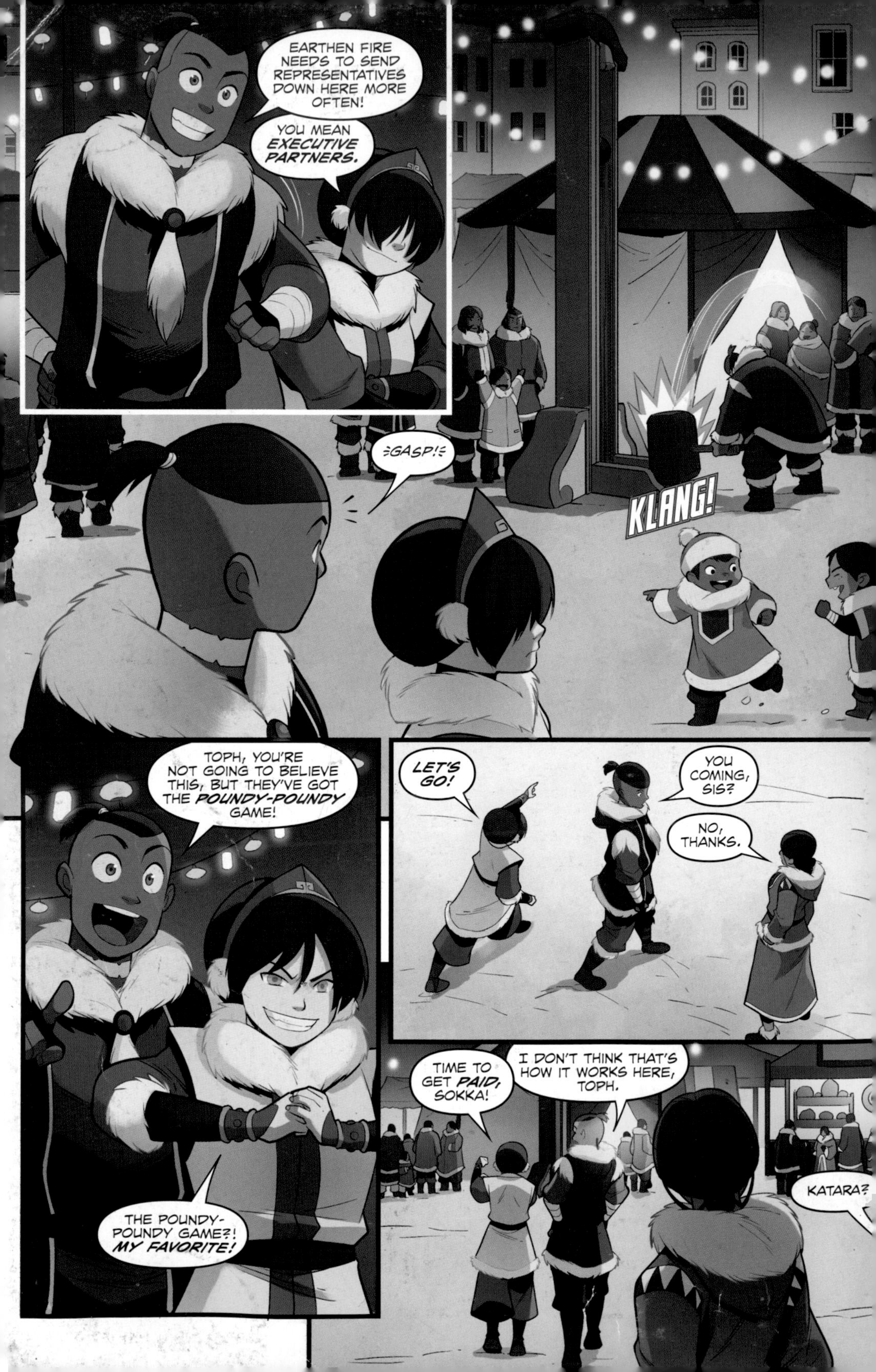
EARTHEN FIRE NEEDS TO SEND REPRESENTATIVES DOWN HERE MORE OFTEN!
YOU MEAN *EXECUTIVE PARTNERS.*
≈GASP!≈
KLANG!
TOPH, YOU'RE NOT GOING TO BELIEVE THIS, BUT THEY'VE GOT THE *POUNDY-POUNDY* GAME!
THE POUNDY-POUNDY GAME?! *MY FAVORITE!*
LET'S GO!
YOU COMING, SIS?
NO, THANKS.
TIME TO GET *PAID,* SOKKA!
I DON'T THINK THAT'S HOW IT WORKS HERE, TOPH.
KATARA?

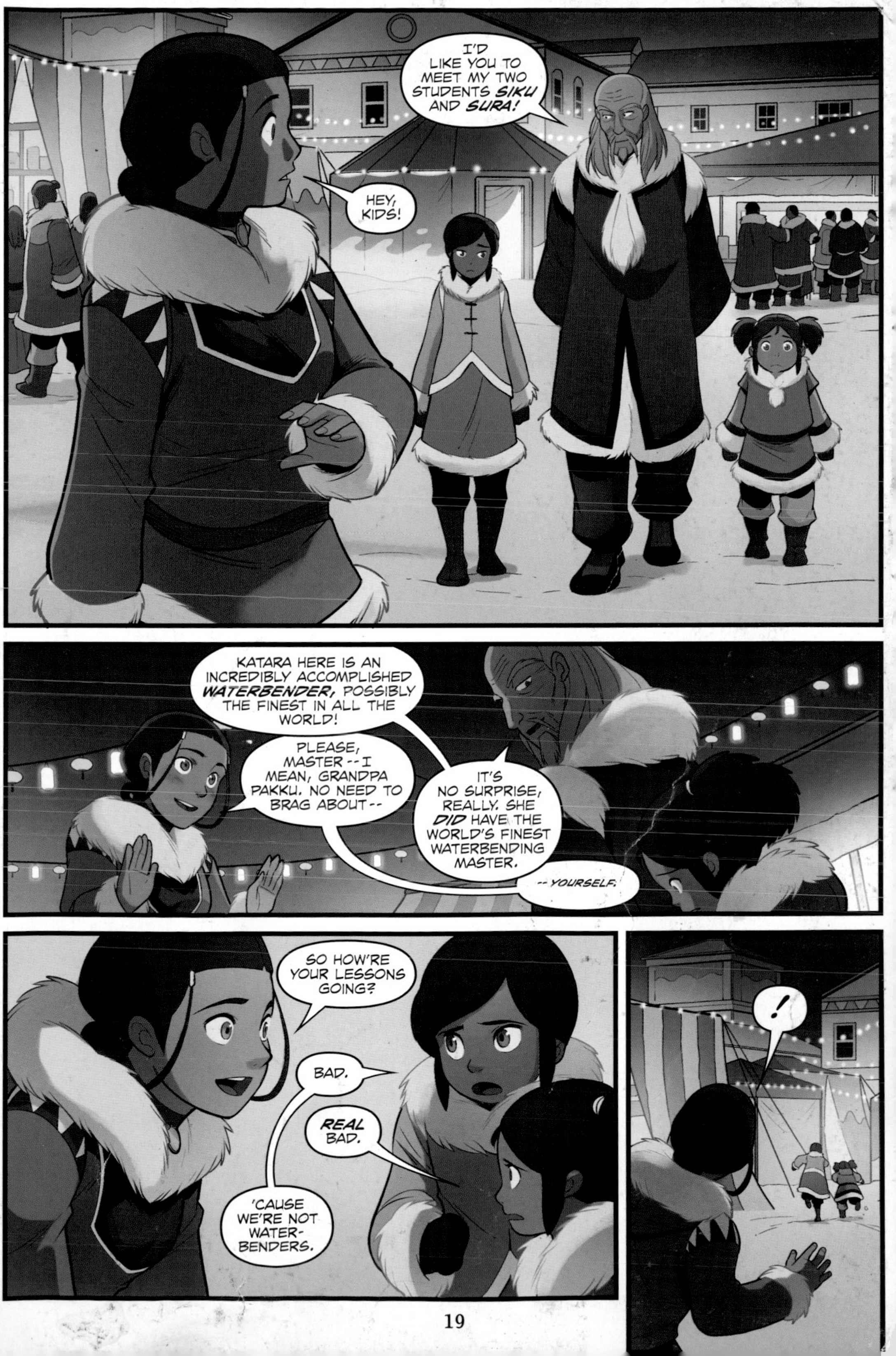
I'D LIKE YOU TO MEET MY TWO STUDENTS SIKU AND SURA!
HEY, KIDS!
KATARA HERE IS AN INCREDIBLY ACCOMPLISHED WATERBENDER, POSSIBLY THE FINEST IN ALL THE WORLD!
PLEASE, MASTER -- I MEAN, GRANDPA PAKKU. NO NEED TO BRAG ABOUT --
IT'S NO SURPRISE, REALLY. SHE DID HAVE THE WORLD'S FINEST WATERBENDING MASTER.
-- YOURSELF.
SO HOW'RE YOUR LESSONS GOING?
BAD.
REAL BAD.
'CAUSE WE'RE NOT WATER-BENDERS.
!

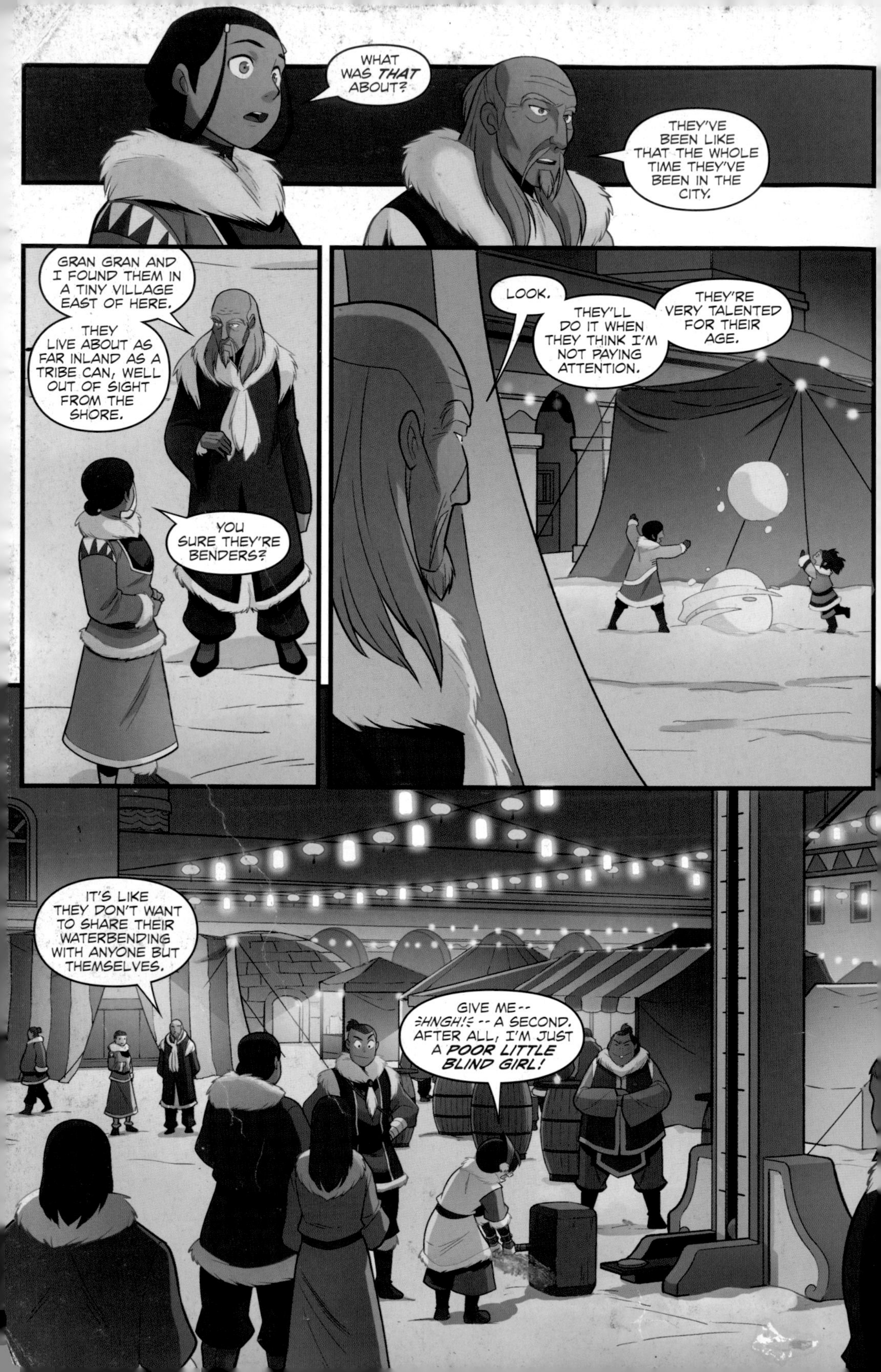
WHAT WAS THAT ABOUT?
THEY'VE BEEN LIKE THAT THE WHOLE TIME THEY'VE BEEN IN THE CITY.
GRAN GRAN AND I FOUND THEM IN A TINY VILLAGE EAST OF HERE.
THEY LIVE ABOUT AS FAR INLAND AS A TRIBE CAN, WELL OUT OF SIGHT FROM THE SHORE.
YOU SURE THEY'RE BENDERS?
LOOK.
THEY'LL DO IT WHEN THEY THINK I'M NOT PAYING ATTENTION.
THEY'RE VERY TALENTED FOR THEIR AGE.
IT'S LIKE THEY DON'T WANT TO SHARE THEIR WATERBENDING WITH ANYONE BUT THEMSELVES.
GIVE ME-- HNGH!! -- A SECOND. AFTER ALL, I'M JUST A POOR LITTLE BLIND GIRL!

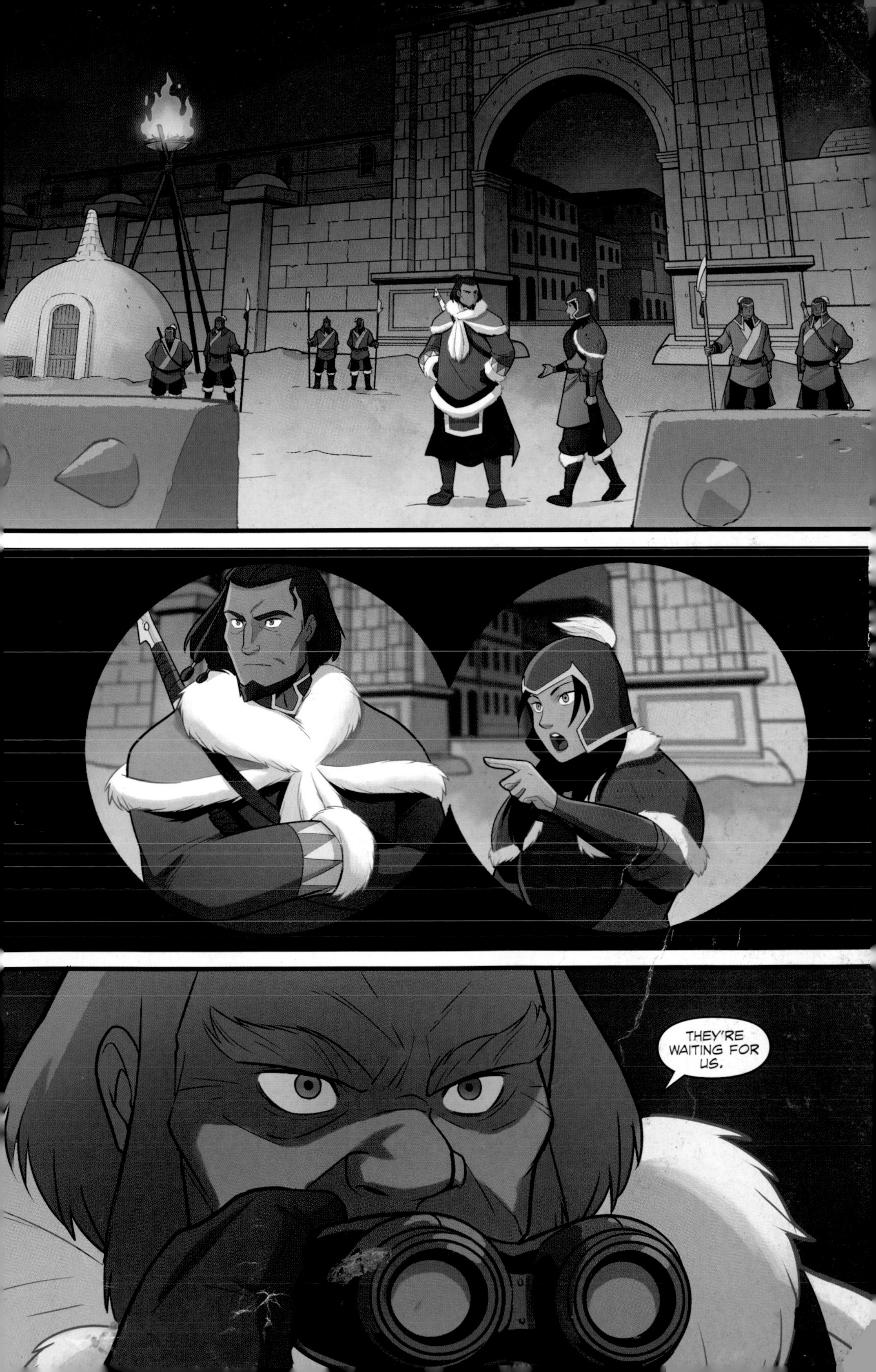
THEY'RE WAITING FOR US.

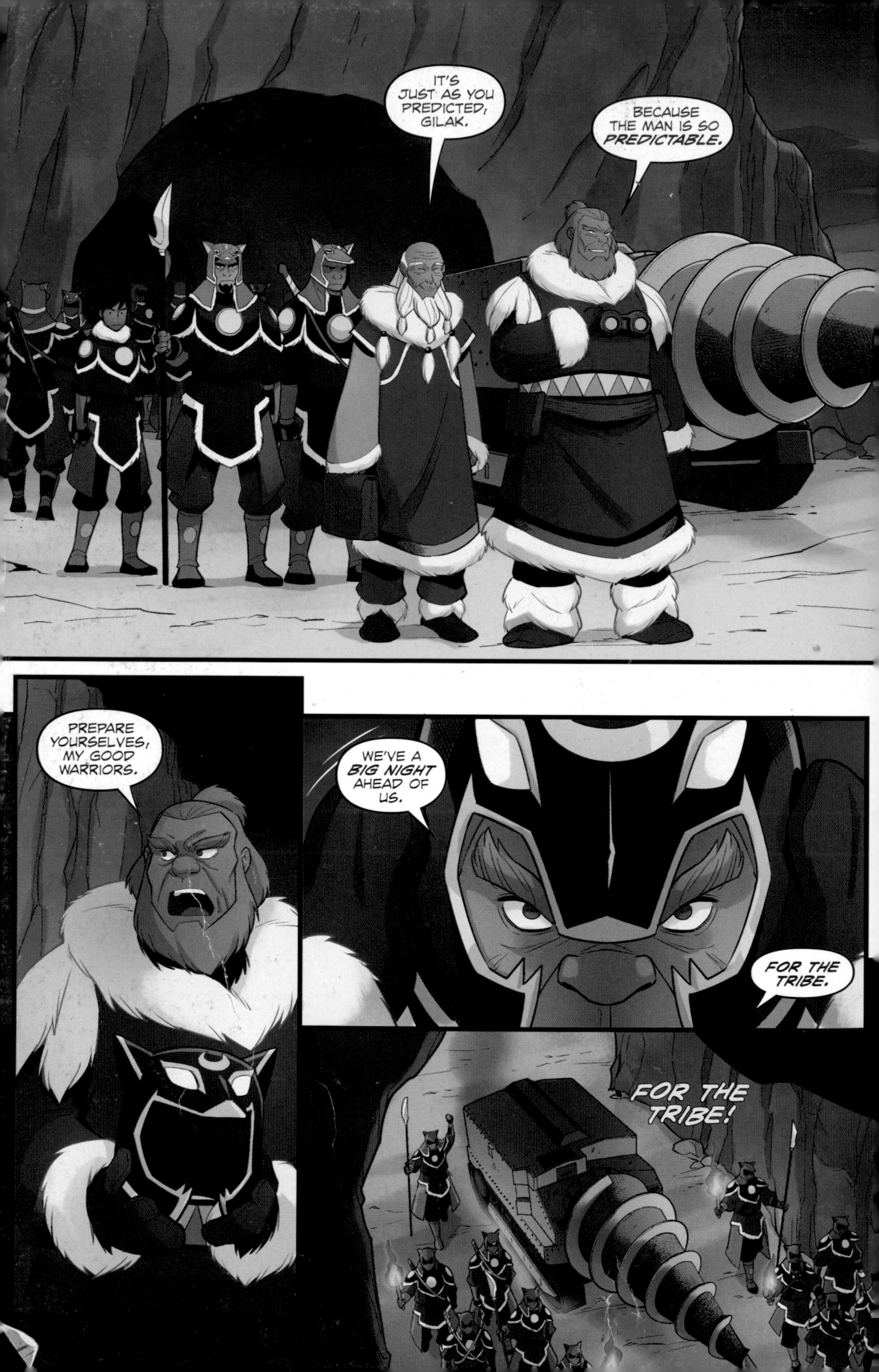
IT'S JUST AS YOU PREDICTED, GILAK.
BECAUSE THE MAN IS SO PREDICTABLE.
PREPARE YOURSELVES, MY GOOD WARRIORS.
WE'VE A BIG NIGHT AHEAD OF US.
FOR THE TRIBE.
FOR THE TRIBE!

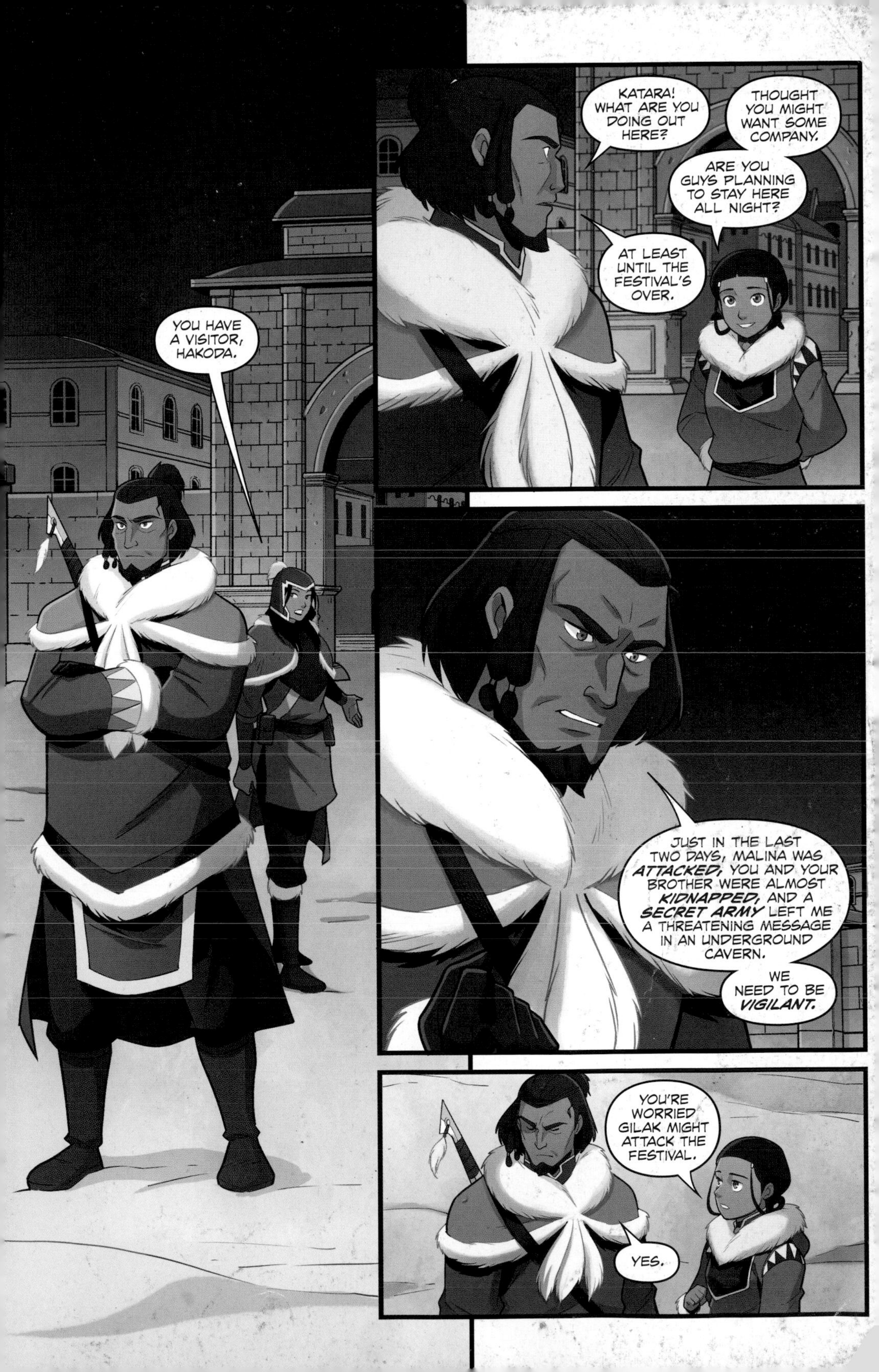
YOU HAVE A VISITOR, HAKODA.
KATARA! WHAT ARE YOU DOING OUT HERE?
THOUGHT YOU MIGHT WANT SOME COMPANY.
ARE YOU GUYS PLANNING TO STAY HERE ALL NIGHT?
AT LEAST UNTIL THE FESTIVAL'S OVER.
JUST IN THE LAST TWO DAYS, MALINA WAS ATTACKED, YOU AND YOUR BROTHER WERE ALMOST KIDNAPPED, AND A SECRET ARMY LEFT ME A THREATENING MESSAGE IN AN UNDERGROUND CAVERN.
WE NEED TO BE VIGILANT.
YOU'RE WORRIED GILAK MIGHT ATTACK THE FESTIVAL.
YES.

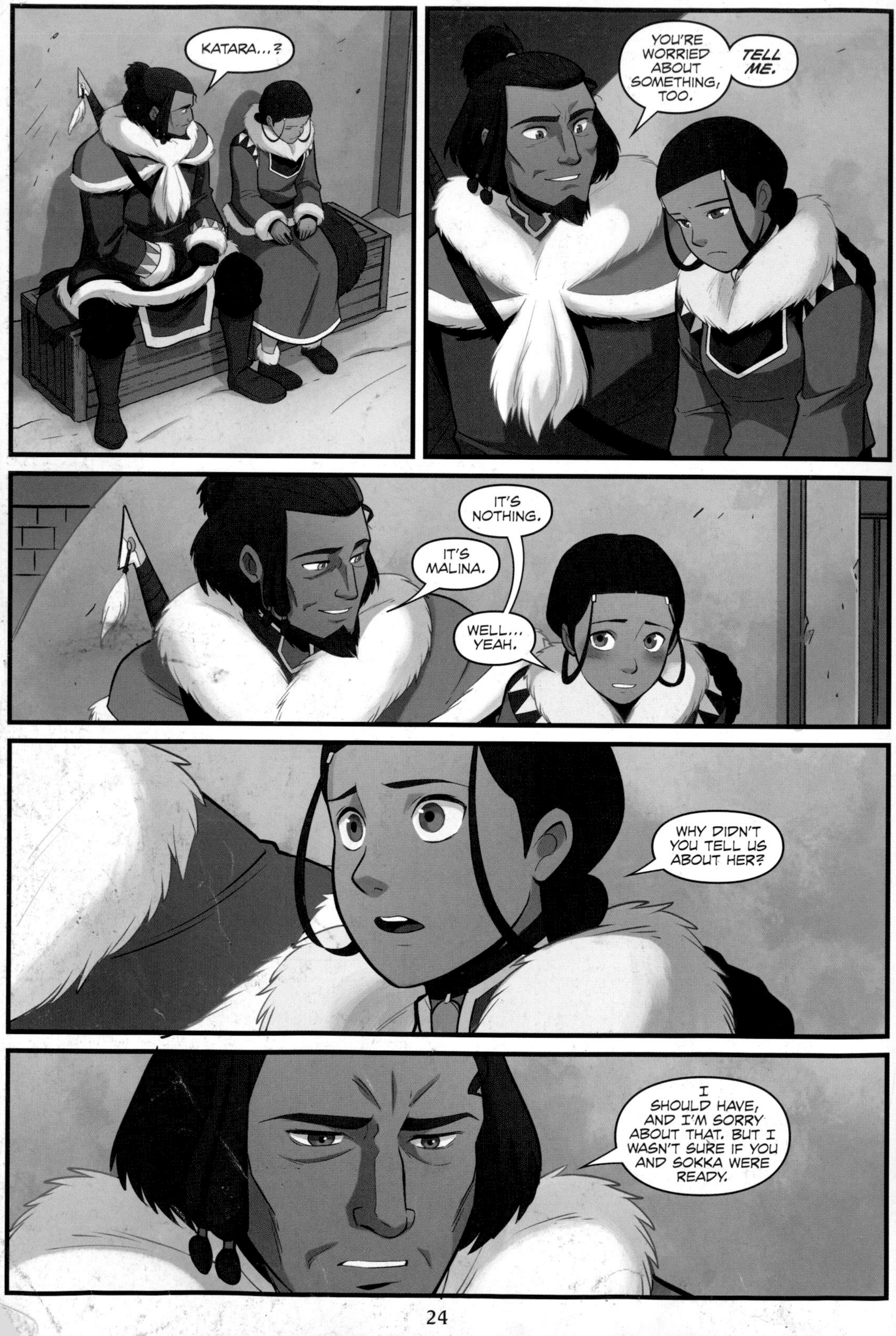
KATARA...?
YOU'RE WORRIED ABOUT SOMETHING, TOO.
TELL ME.
IT'S MALINA.
IT'S NOTHING.
WELL... YEAH.
WHY DIDN'T YOU TELL US ABOUT HER?
I SHOULD HAVE, AND I'M SORRY ABOUT THAT. BUT I WASN'T SURE IF YOU AND SOKKA WERE READY.

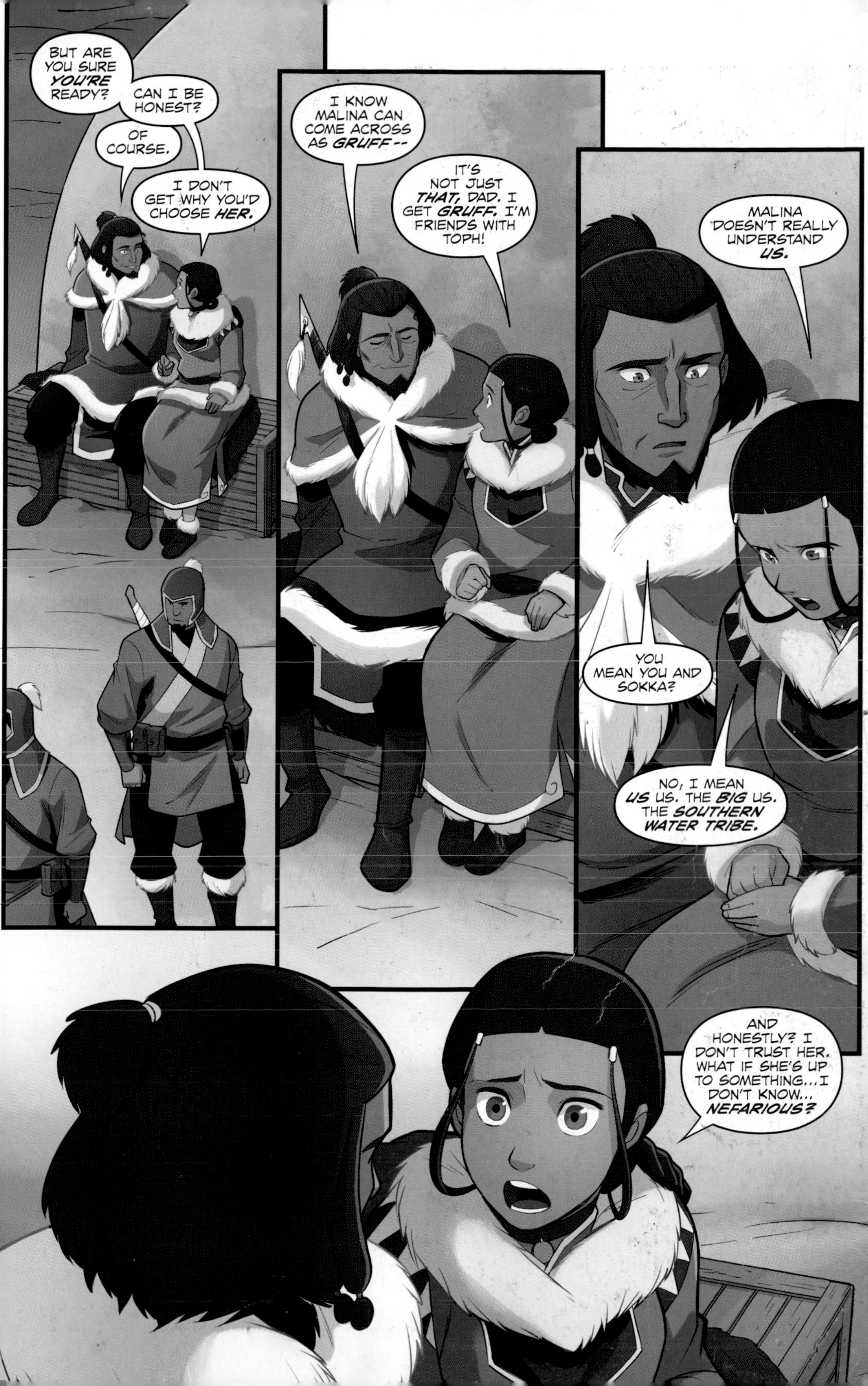
BUT ARE YOU SURE *YOU'RE* READY?
CAN I BE HONEST?
OF COURSE.
I DON'T GET WHY YOU'D CHOOSE *HER.*
I KNOW MALINA CAN COME ACROSS AS *GRUFF*--
IT'S NOT JUST *THAT,* DAD. I GET *GRUFF.* I'M FRIENDS WITH TOPH!
MALINA DOESN'T REALLY UNDERSTAND *US.*
YOU MEAN YOU AND SOKKA?
NO, I MEAN *US* US. THE *BIG* US. THE *SOUTHERN WATER TRIBE.*
AND HONESTLY? I DON'T TRUST HER. WHAT IF SHE'S UP TO SOMETHING... I DON'T KNOW... *NEFARIOUS?*

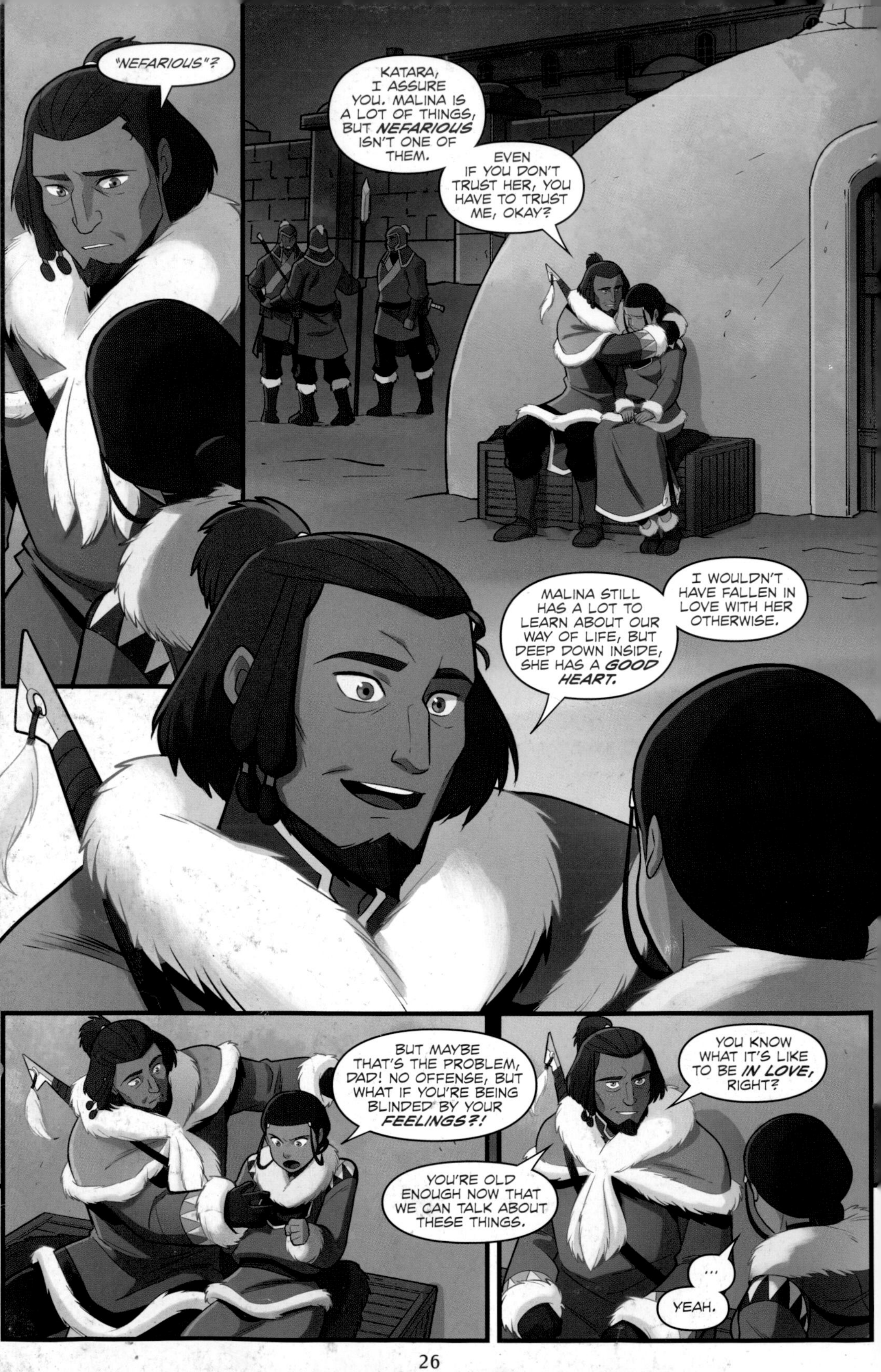
"NEFARIOUS"?
KATARA, I ASSURE YOU. MALINA IS A LOT OF THINGS, BUT NEFARIOUS ISN'T ONE OF THEM.
EVEN IF YOU DON'T TRUST HER, YOU HAVE TO TRUST ME, OKAY?
MALINA STILL HAS A LOT TO LEARN ABOUT OUR WAY OF LIFE, BUT DEEP DOWN INSIDE, SHE HAS A GOOD HEART.
I WOULDN'T HAVE FALLEN IN LOVE WITH HER OTHERWISE.
BUT MAYBE THAT'S THE PROBLEM, DAD! NO OFFENSE, BUT WHAT IF YOU'RE BEING BLINDED BY YOUR FEELINGS?!
YOU'RE OLD ENOUGH NOW THAT WE CAN TALK ABOUT THESE THINGS.
YOU KNOW WHAT IT'S LIKE TO BE IN LOVE, RIGHT?
...
YEAH.

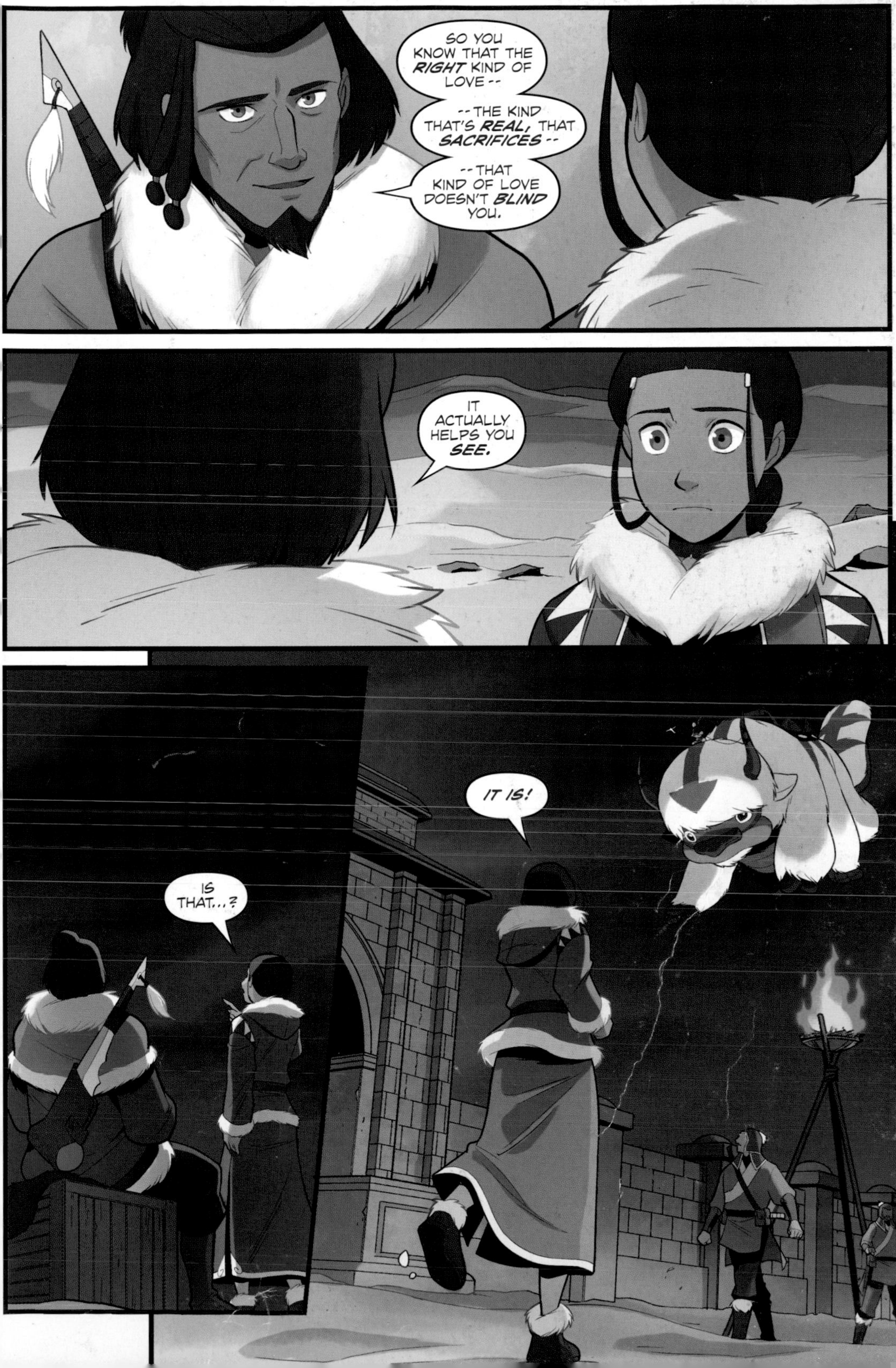
SO YOU KNOW THAT THE RIGHT KIND OF LOVE --
-- THE KIND THAT'S REAL, THAT SACRIFICES --
-- THAT KIND OF LOVE DOESN'T BLIND YOU.
IT ACTUALLY HELPS YOU SEE.
IS THAT...?
IT IS!

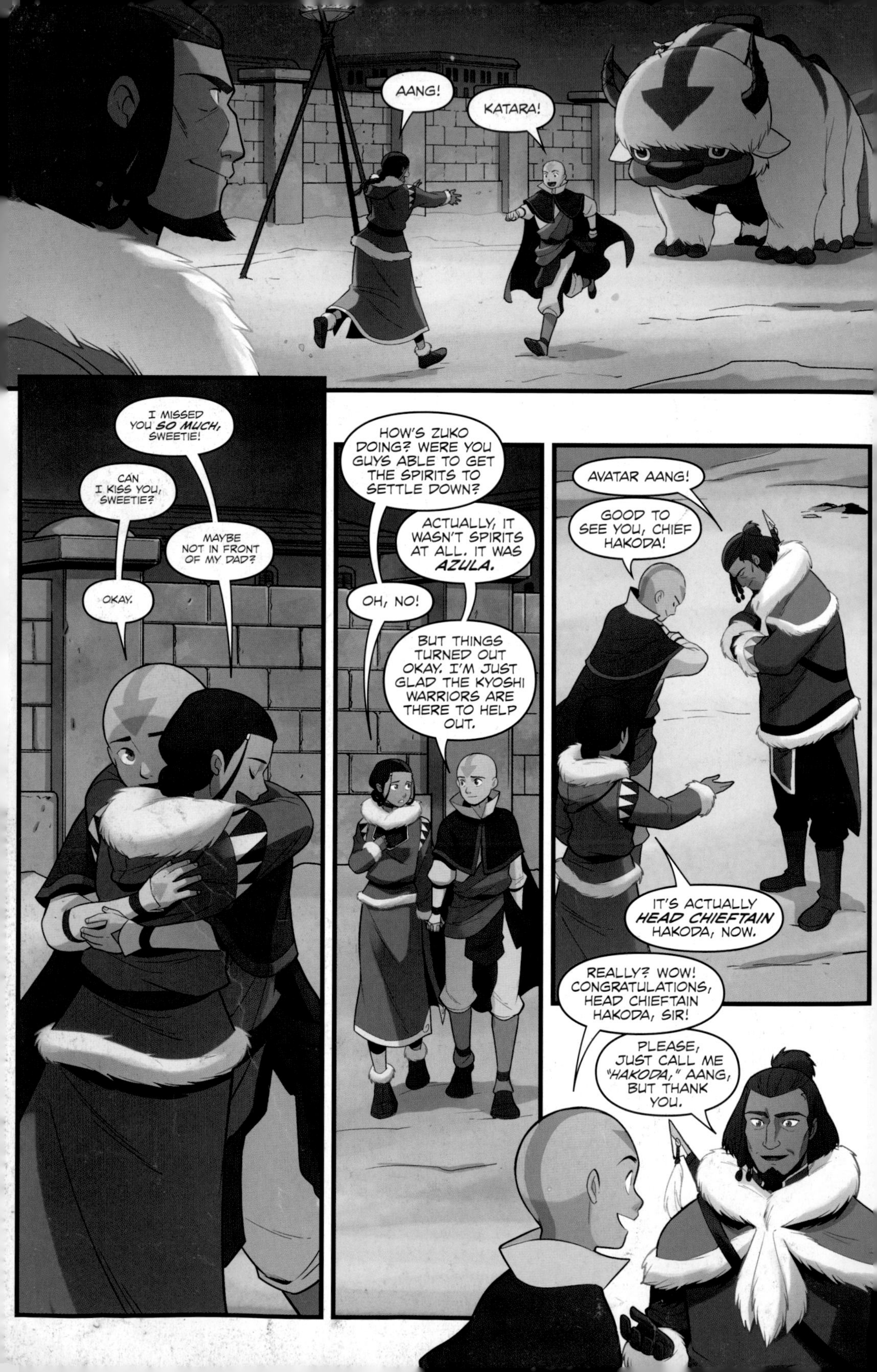
AANG!
KATARA!
I MISSED YOU SO MUCH, SWEETIE!
CAN I KISS YOU, SWEETIE?
MAYBE NOT IN FRONT OF MY DAD?
OKAY.
HOW'S ZUKO DOING? WERE YOU GUYS ABLE TO GET THE SPIRITS TO SETTLE DOWN?
ACTUALLY, IT WASN'T SPIRITS AT ALL. IT WAS AZULA.
OH, NO!
BUT THINGS TURNED OUT OKAY. I'M JUST GLAD THE KYOSHI WARRIORS ARE THERE TO HELP OUT.
AVATAR AANG!
GOOD TO SEE YOU, CHIEF HAKODA!
IT'S ACTUALLY HEAD CHIEFTAIN HAKODA, NOW.
REALLY? WOW! CONGRATULATIONS, HEAD CHIEFTAIN HAKODA, SIR!
PLEASE, JUST CALL ME "HAKODA," AANG, BUT THANK YOU.

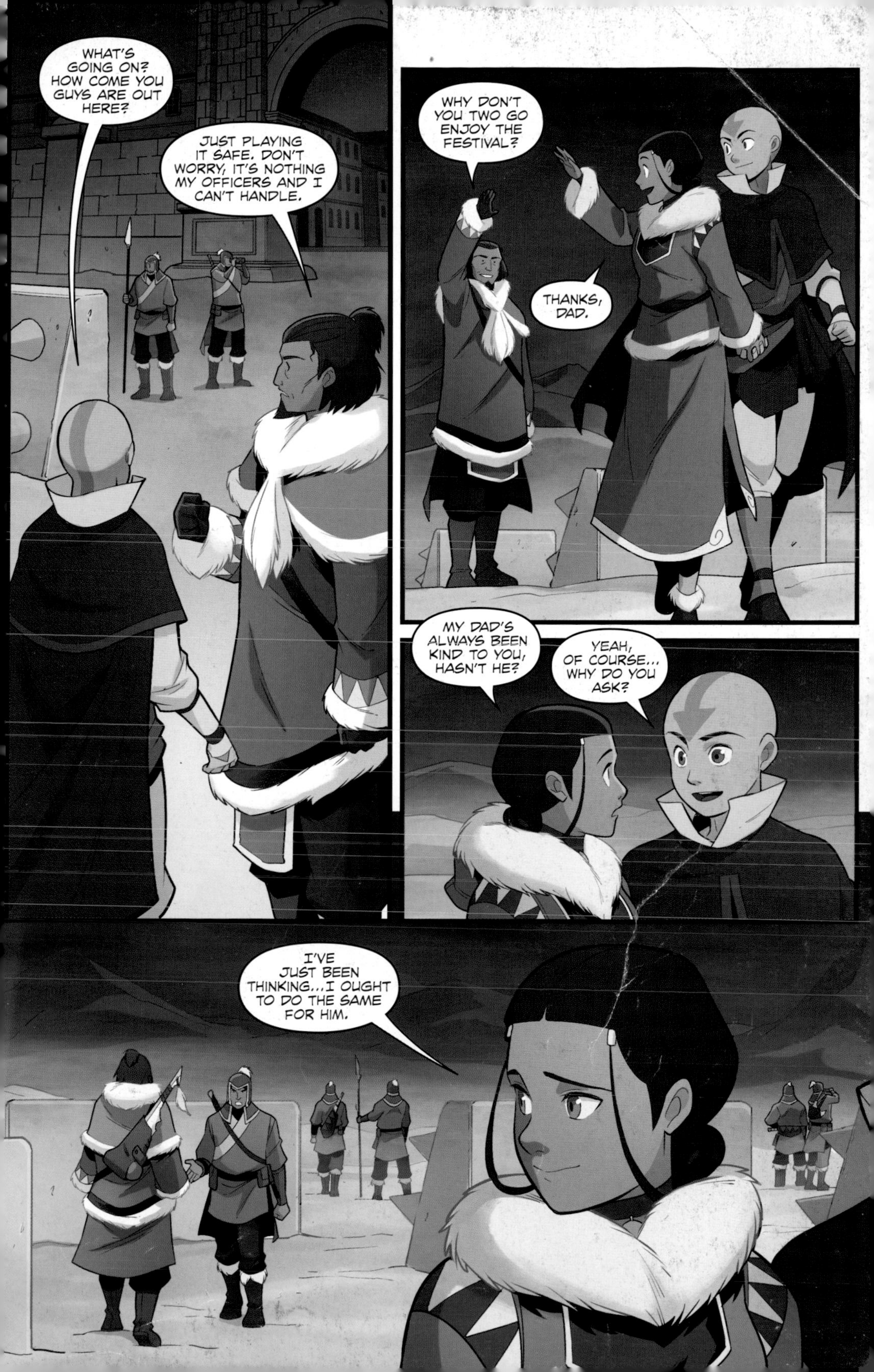
WHAT'S GOING ON? HOW COME YOU GUYS ARE OUT HERE?
JUST PLAYING IT SAFE. DON'T WORRY, IT'S NOTHING MY OFFICERS AND I CAN'T HANDLE.
WHY DON'T YOU TWO GO ENJOY THE FESTIVAL?
THANKS, DAD.
MY DAD'S ALWAYS BEEN KIND TO YOU, HASN'T HE?
YEAH, OF COURSE... WHY DO YOU ASK?
I'VE JUST BEEN THINKING... I OUGHT TO DO THE SAME FOR HIM.

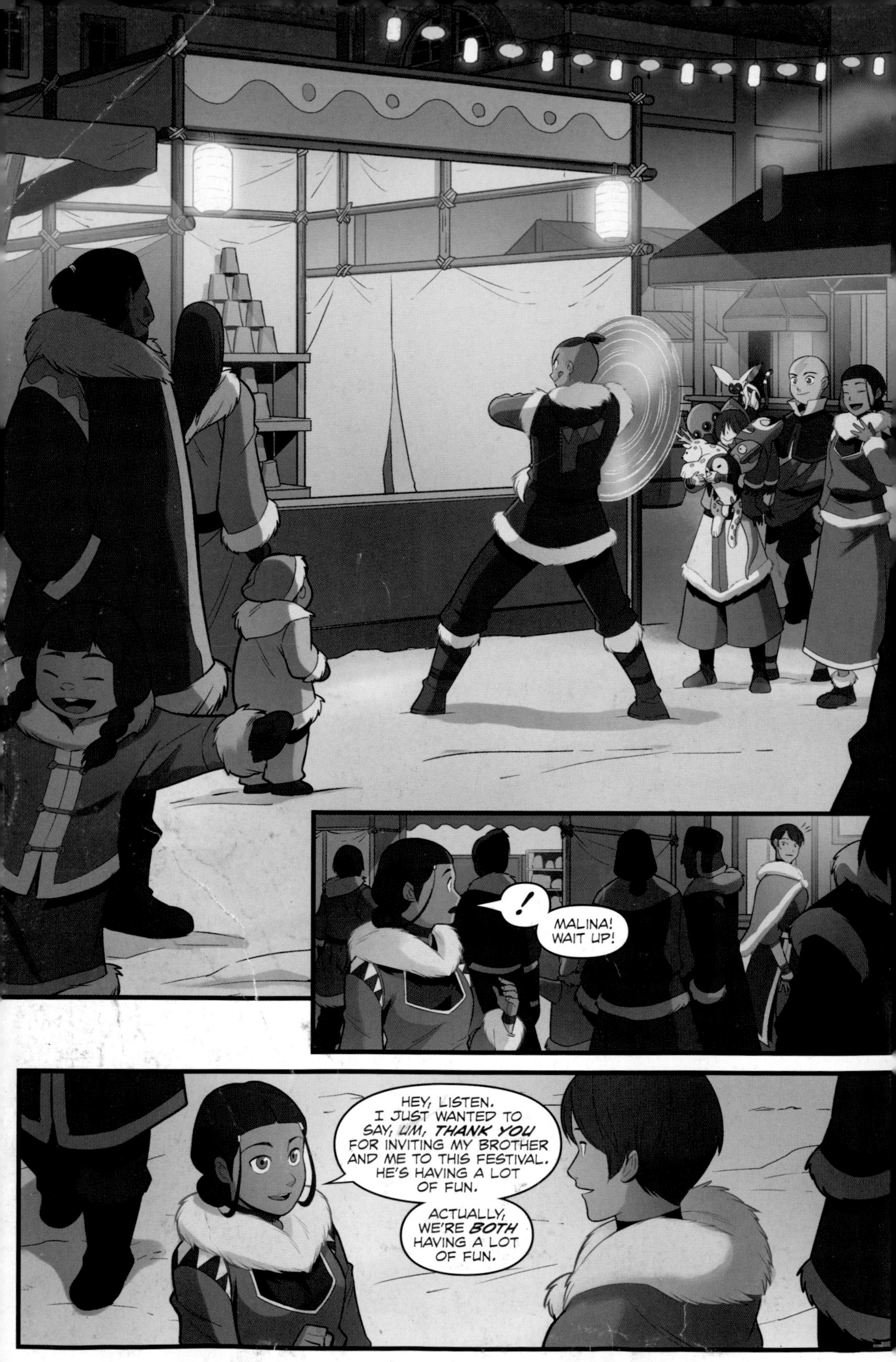
!
MALINA! WAIT UP!
HEY, LISTEN. I JUST WANTED TO SAY, UM, THANK YOU FOR INVITING MY BROTHER AND ME TO THIS FESTIVAL. HE'S HAVING A LOT OF FUN.
ACTUALLY, WE'RE BOTH HAVING A LOT OF FUN.

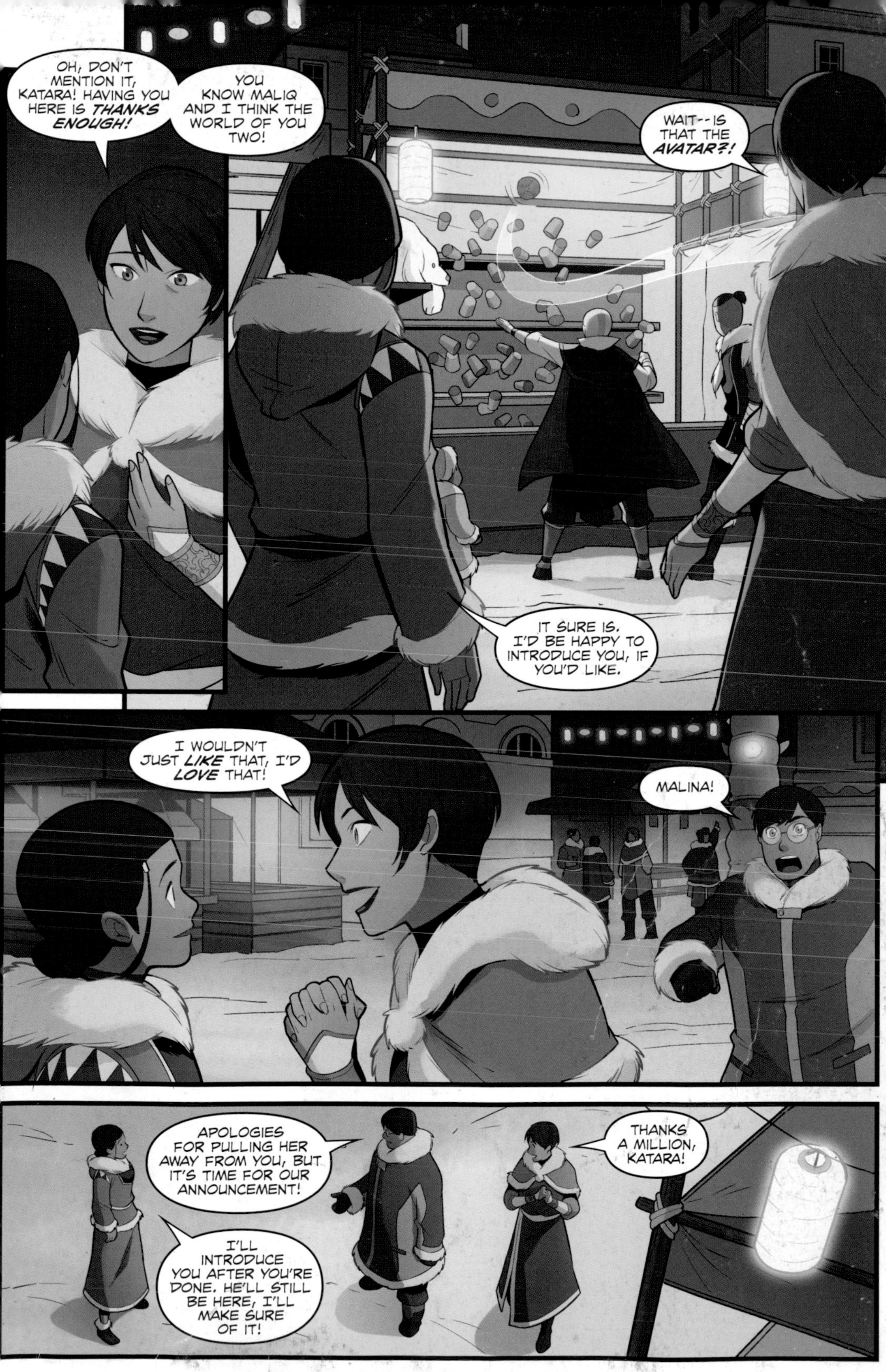
OH, DON'T MENTION IT, KATARA! HAVING YOU HERE IS THANKS ENOUGH!
YOU KNOW MALIQ AND I THINK THE WORLD OF YOU TWO!
WAIT--IS THAT THE AVATAR?!
IT SURE IS. I'D BE HAPPY TO INTRODUCE YOU, IF YOU'D LIKE.
I WOULDN'T JUST LIKE THAT, I'D LOVE THAT!
MALINA!
APOLOGIES FOR PULLING HER AWAY FROM YOU, BUT IT'S TIME FOR OUR ANNOUNCEMENT!
THANKS A MILLION, KATARA!
I'LL INTRODUCE YOU AFTER YOU'RE DONE. HE'LL STILL BE HERE, I'LL MAKE SURE OF IT!

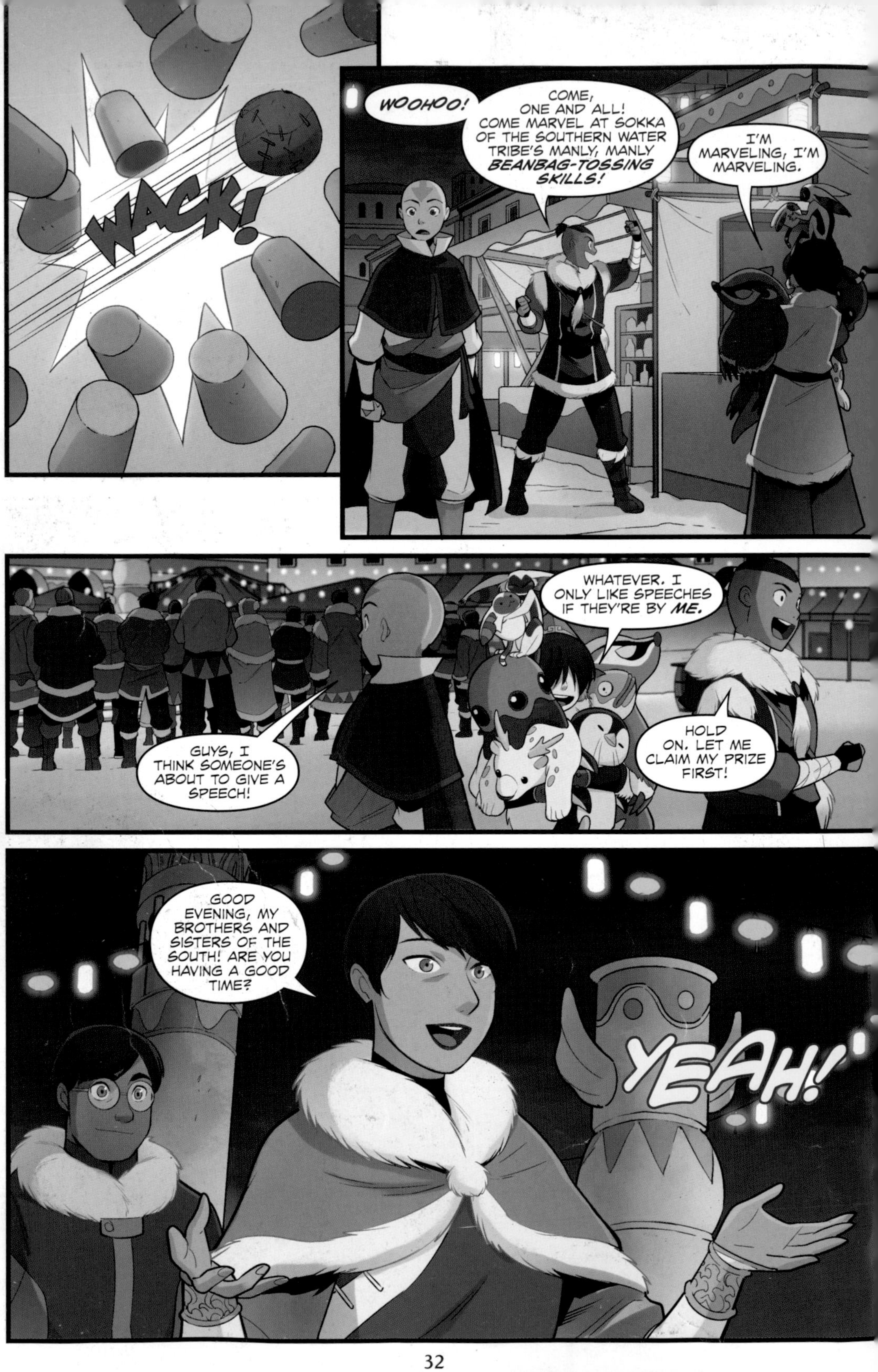
WACK!
WOOHOO!
COME, ONE AND ALL! COME MARVEL AT SOKKA OF THE SOUTHERN WATER TRIBE'S MANLY, MANLY BEANBAG-TOSSING SKILLS!
I'M MARVELING, I'M MARVELING.
GUYS, I THINK SOMEONE'S ABOUT TO GIVE A SPEECH!
WHATEVER. I ONLY LIKE SPEECHES IF THEY'RE BY ME.
HOLD ON. LET ME CLAIM MY PRIZE FIRST!
GOOD EVENING, MY BROTHERS AND SISTERS OF THE SOUTH! ARE YOU HAVING A GOOD TIME?
YEAH!

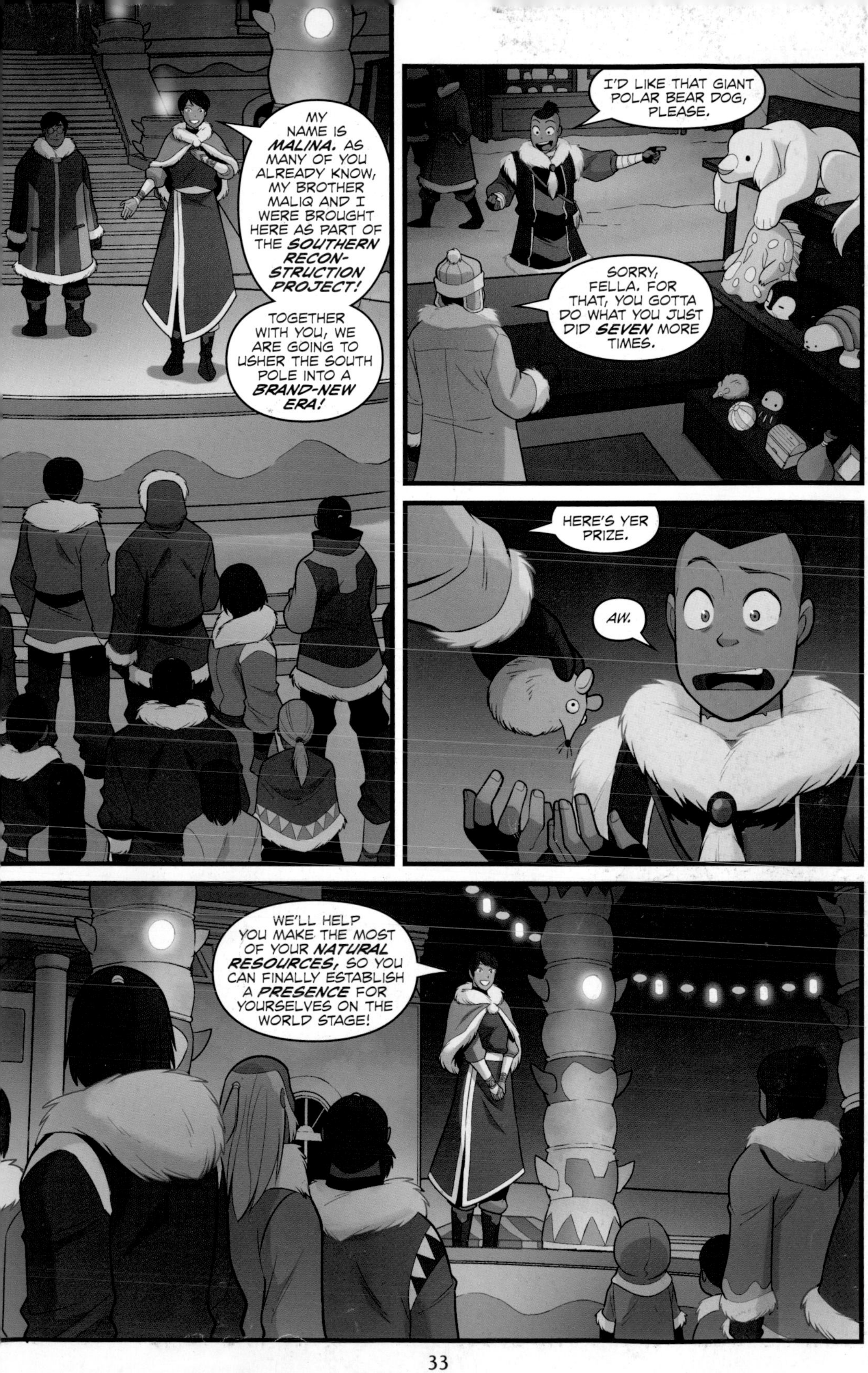
MY NAME IS MALINA. AS MANY OF YOU ALREADY KNOW, MY BROTHER MALIQ AND I WERE BROUGHT HERE AS PART OF THE SOUTHERN RECON-STRUCTION PROJECT!
TOGETHER WITH YOU, WE ARE GOING TO USHER THE SOUTH POLE INTO A BRAND-NEW ERA!
I'D LIKE THAT GIANT POLAR BEAR DOG, PLEASE.
SORRY, FELLA. FOR THAT, YOU GOTTA DO WHAT YOU JUST DID SEVEN MORE TIMES.
HERE'S YER PRIZE.
AW.
WE'LL HELP YOU MAKE THE MOST OF YOUR NATURAL RESOURCES, SO YOU CAN FINALLY ESTABLISH A PRESENCE FOR YOURSELVES ON THE WORLD STAGE!

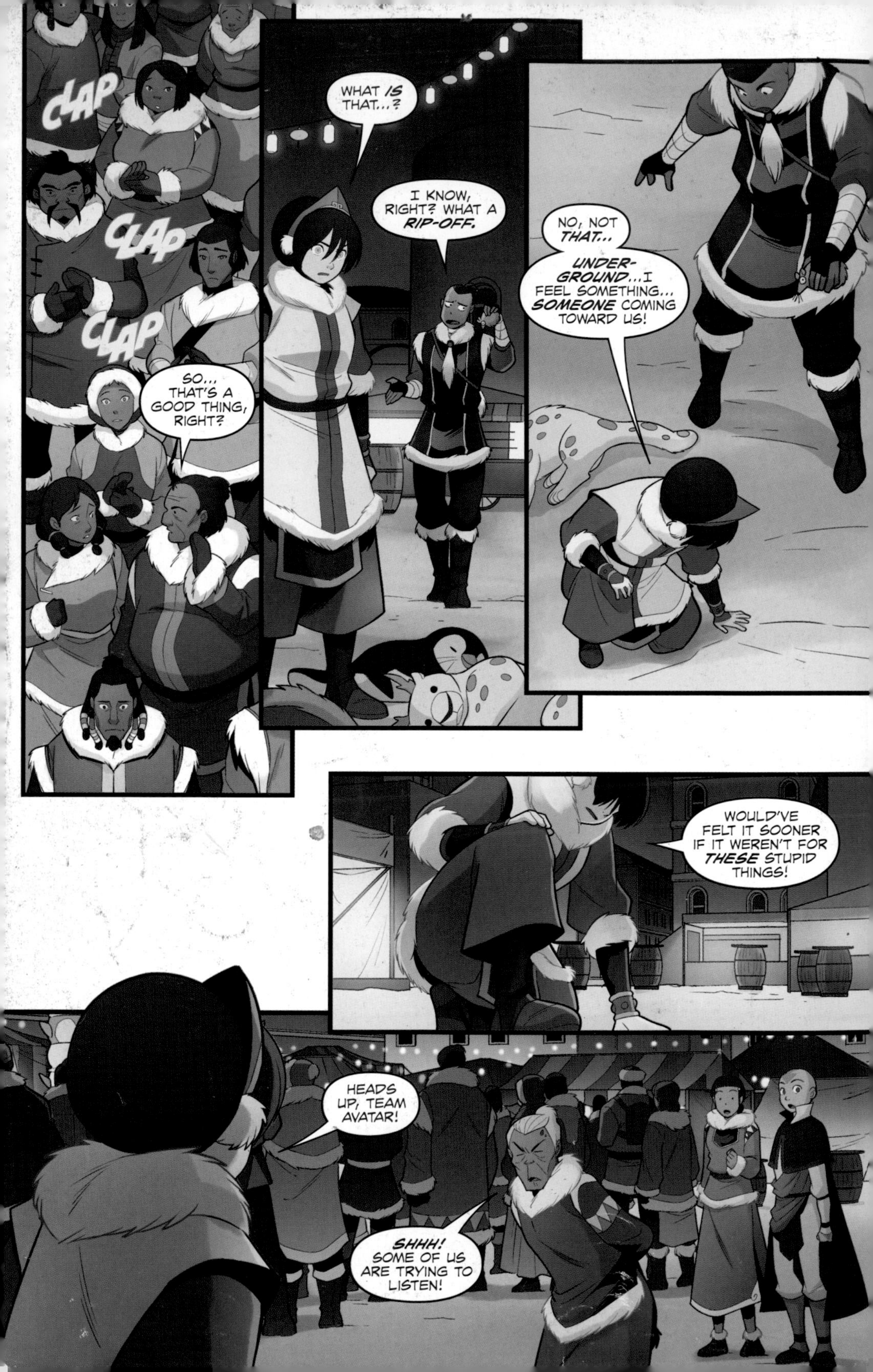
CLAP
CLAP
CLAP
SO... THAT'S A GOOD THING, RIGHT?
WHAT IS THAT...?
I KNOW, RIGHT? WHAT A RIP-OFF.
NO, NOT THAT...
UNDER-GROUND...I FEEL SOMETHING... SOMEONE COMING TOWARD US!
WOULD'VE FELT IT SOONER IF IT WEREN'T FOR THESE STUPID THINGS!
HEADS UP, TEAM AVATAR!
SHHH! SOME OF US ARE TRYING TO LISTEN!

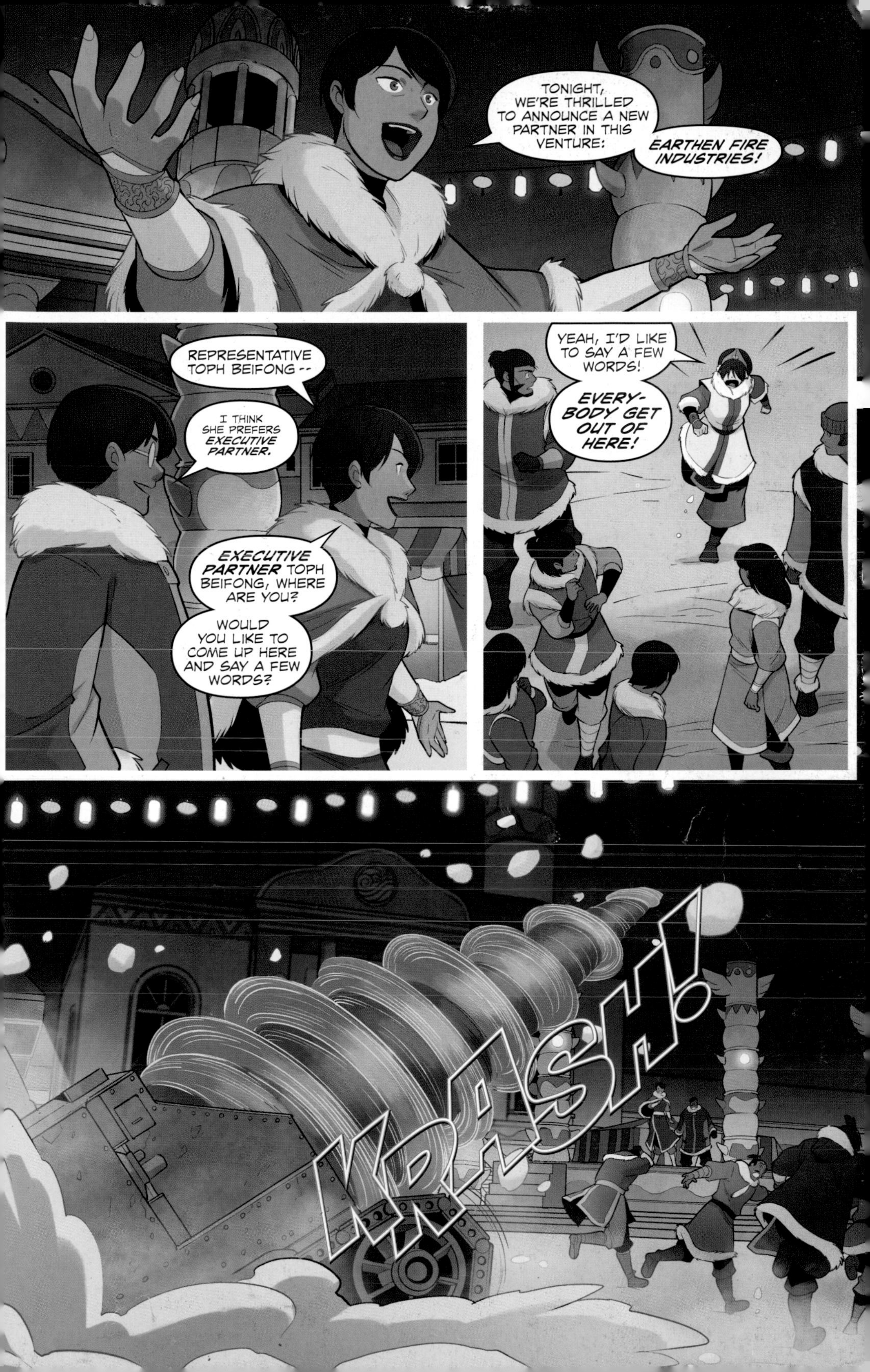
TONIGHT, WE'RE THRILLED TO ANNOUNCE A NEW PARTNER IN THIS VENTURE:
EARTHEN FIRE INDUSTRIES!
REPRESENTATIVE TOPH BEIFONG --
I THINK SHE PREFERS EXECUTIVE PARTNER.
EXECUTIVE PARTNER TOPH BEIFONG, WHERE ARE YOU?
WOULD YOU LIKE TO COME UP HERE AND SAY A FEW WORDS?
YEAH, I'D LIKE TO SAY A FEW WORDS!
EVERY-BODY GET OUT OF HERE!
KRASH!

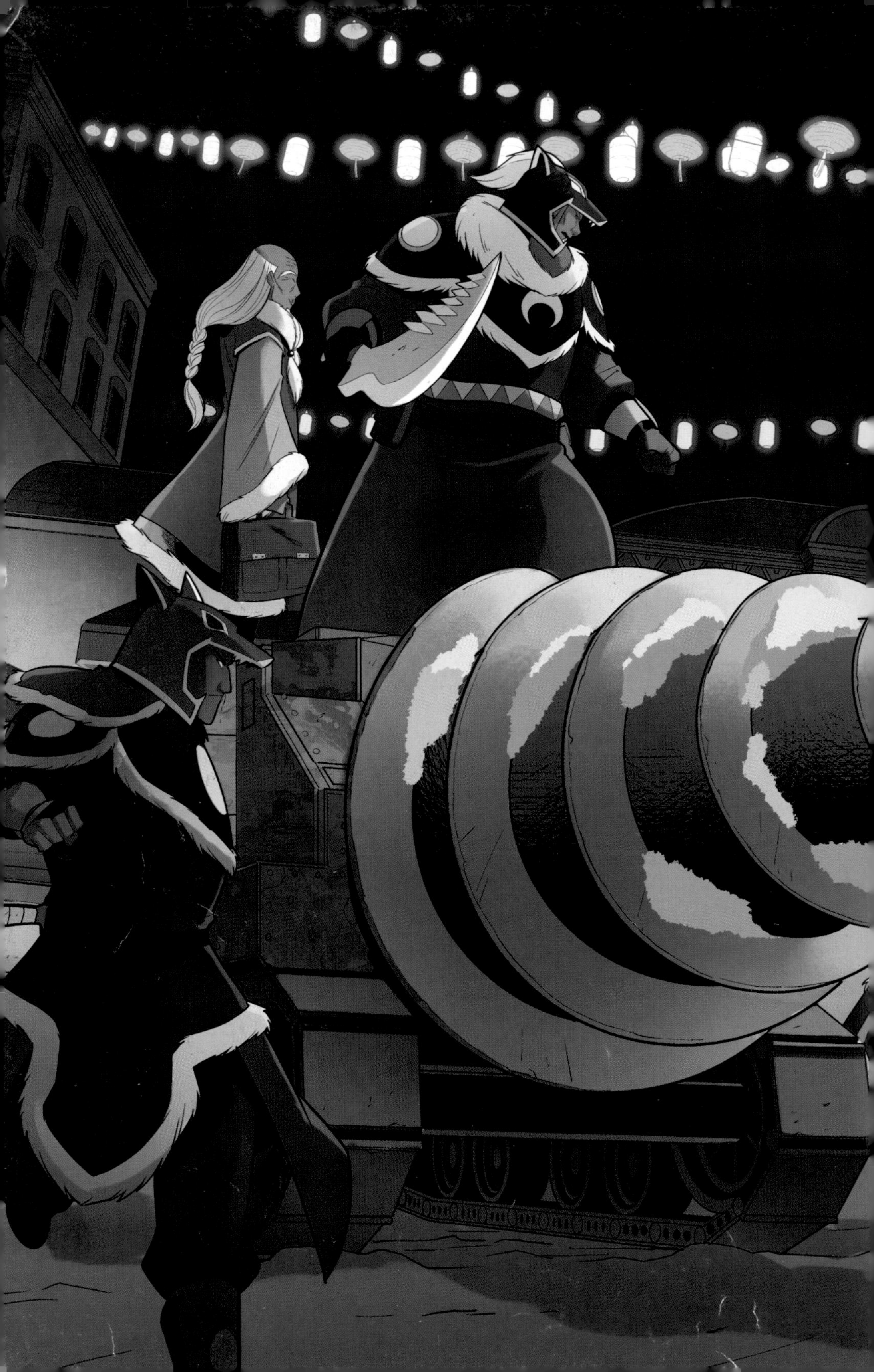

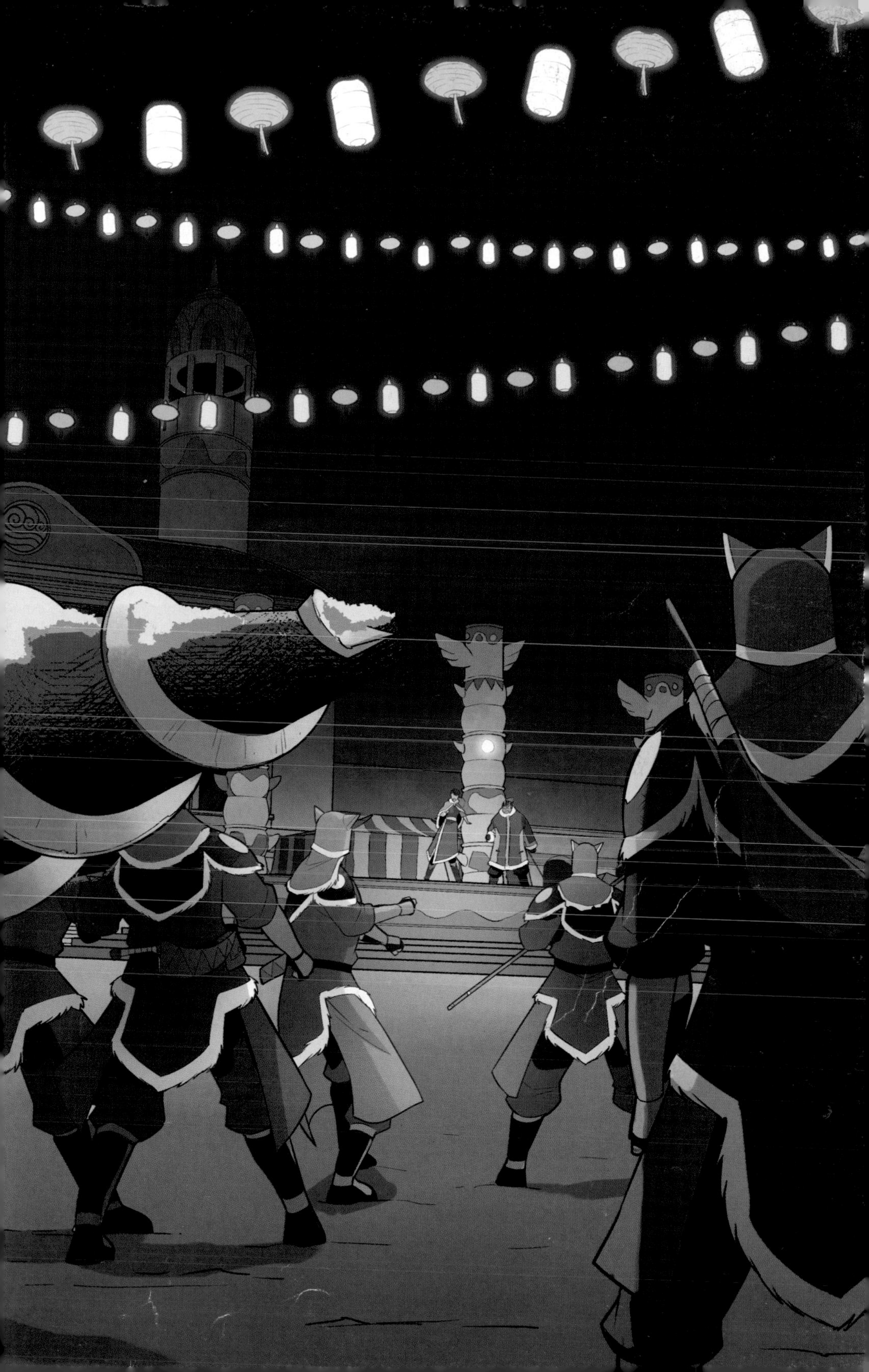

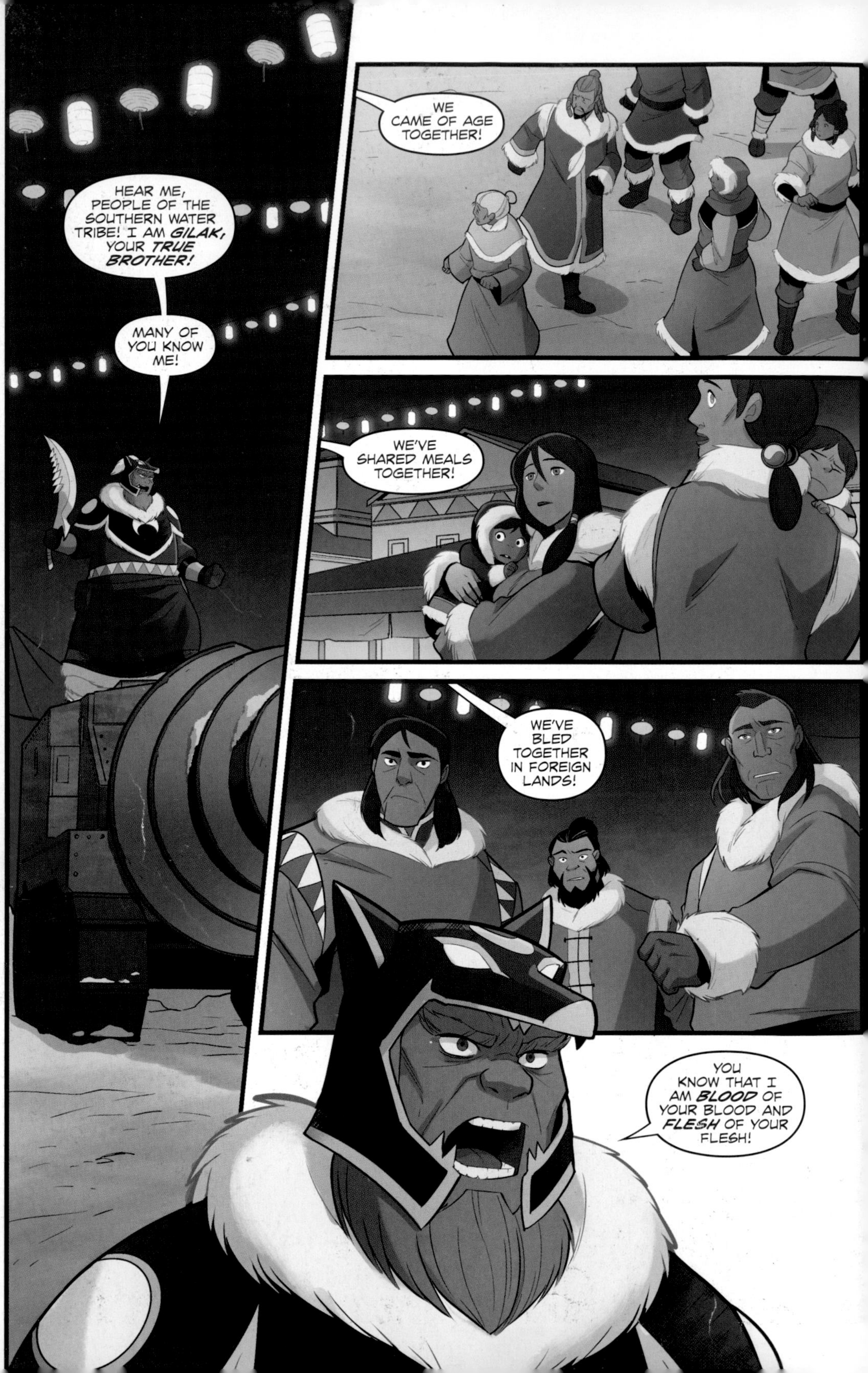

HEAR ME, PEOPLE OF THE SOUTHERN WATER TRIBE! I AM GILAK, YOUR TRUE BROTHER!
MANY OF YOU KNOW ME!
WE CAME OF AGE TOGETHER!
WE'VE SHARED MEALS TOGETHER!
WE'VE BLED TOGETHER IN FOREIGN LANDS!
YOU KNOW THAT I AM BLOOD OF YOUR BLOOD AND FLESH OF YOUR FLESH!

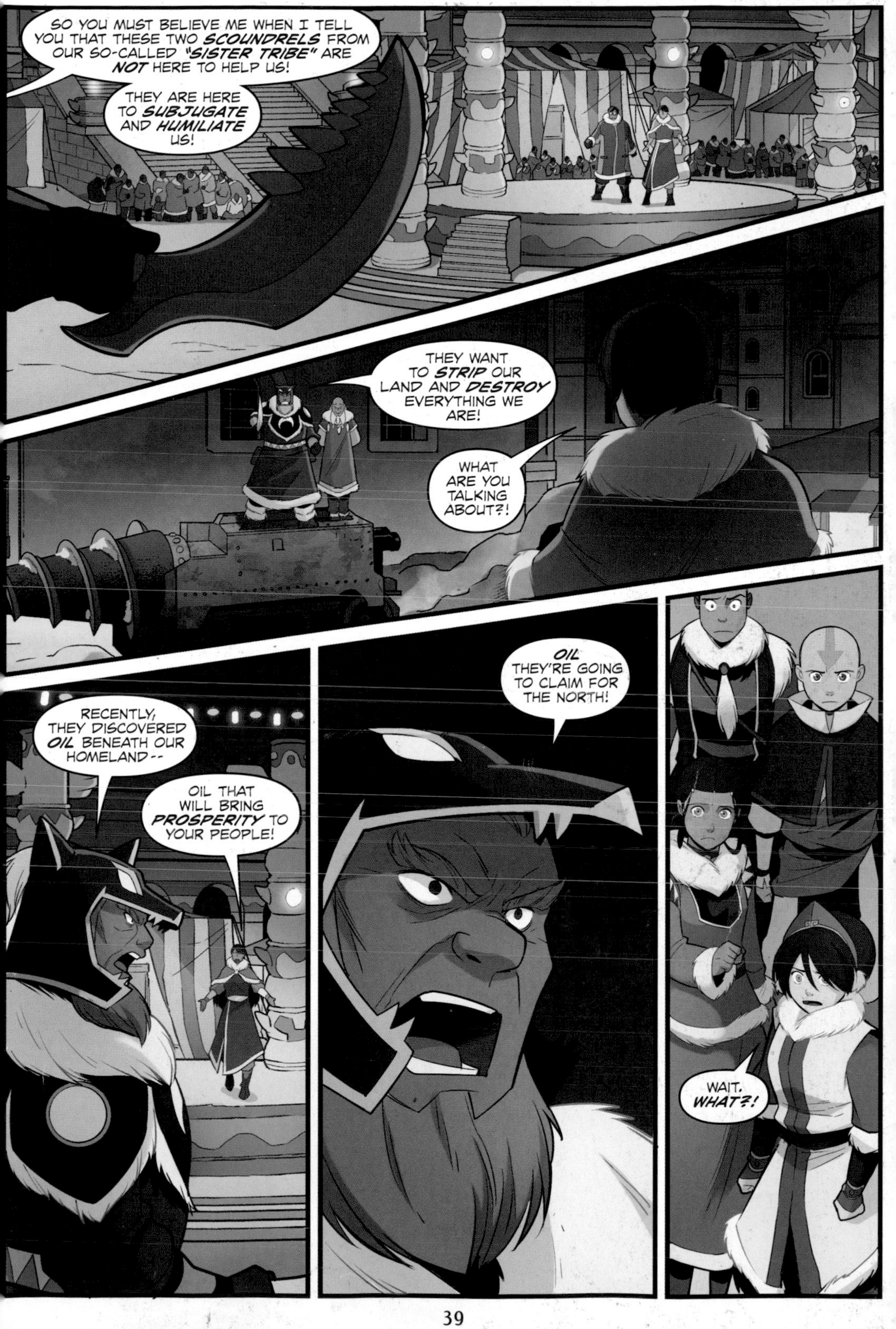

SO YOU MUST BELIEVE ME WHEN I TELL YOU THAT THESE TWO SCOUNDRELS FROM OUR SO-CALLED "SISTER TRIBE" ARE NOT HERE TO HELP US!
THEY ARE HERE TO SUBJUGATE AND HUMILIATE US!
THEY WANT TO STRIP OUR LAND AND DESTROY EVERYTHING WE ARE!
WHAT ARE YOU TALKING ABOUT?!
RECENTLY, THEY DISCOVERED OIL BENEATH OUR HOMELAND--
OIL THAT WILL BRING PROSPERITY TO YOUR PEOPLE!
OIL THEY'RE GOING TO CLAIM FOR THE NORTH!
WAIT. WHAT?!

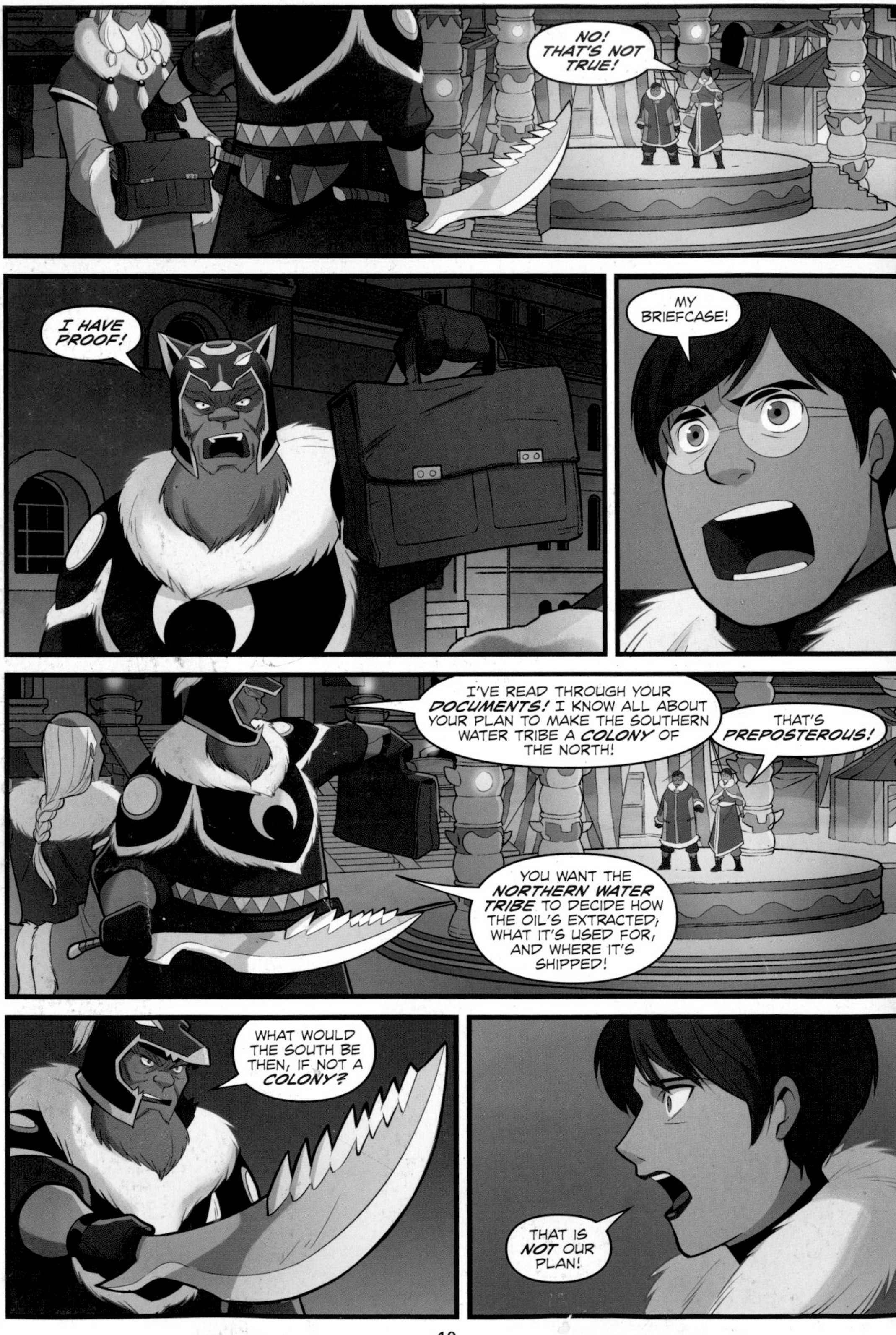
NO! THAT'S NOT TRUE!
I HAVE PROOF!
MY BRIEFCASE!
I'VE READ THROUGH YOUR DOCUMENTS! I KNOW ALL ABOUT YOUR PLAN TO MAKE THE SOUTHERN WATER TRIBE A COLONY OF THE NORTH!
THAT'S PREPOSTEROUS!
YOU WANT THE NORTHERN WATER TRIBE TO DECIDE HOW THE OIL'S EXTRACTED; WHAT IT'S USED FOR, AND WHERE IT'S SHIPPED!
WHAT WOULD THE SOUTH BE THEN, IF NOT A COLONY?
THAT IS NOT OUR PLAN!

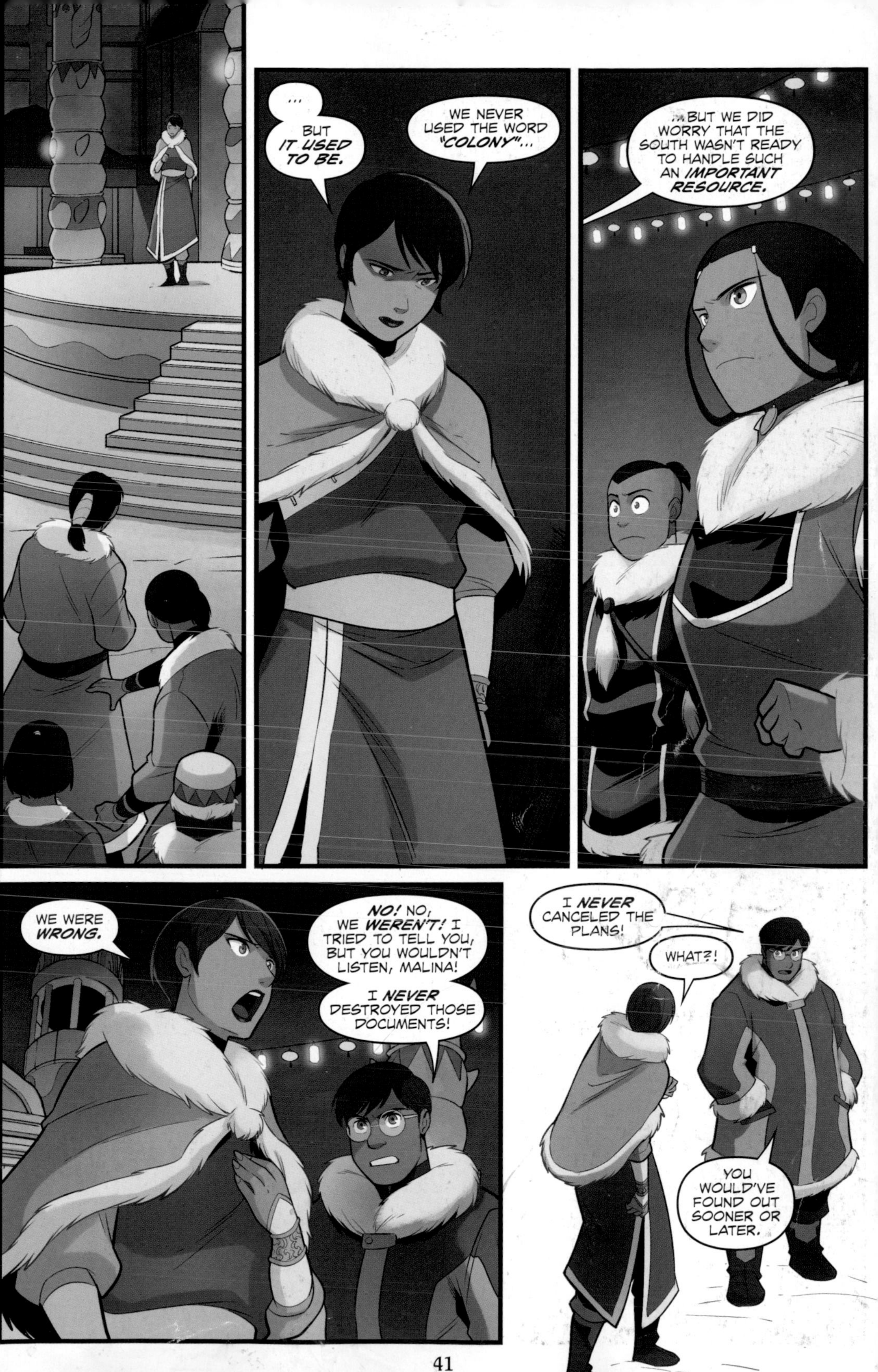
...
BUT *IT USED TO BE.*
WE NEVER USED THE WORD *"COLONY"*...
...BUT WE DID WORRY THAT THE SOUTH WASN'T READY TO HANDLE SUCH AN *IMPORTANT RESOURCE.*
WE WERE *WRONG.*
NO! NO, WE *WEREN'T!* I TRIED TO TELL YOU, BUT YOU WOULDN'T LISTEN, MALINA!
I *NEVER* DESTROYED THOSE DOCUMENTS!
I *NEVER* CANCELED THE PLANS!
WHAT?!
YOU WOULD'VE FOUND OUT SOONER OR LATER.

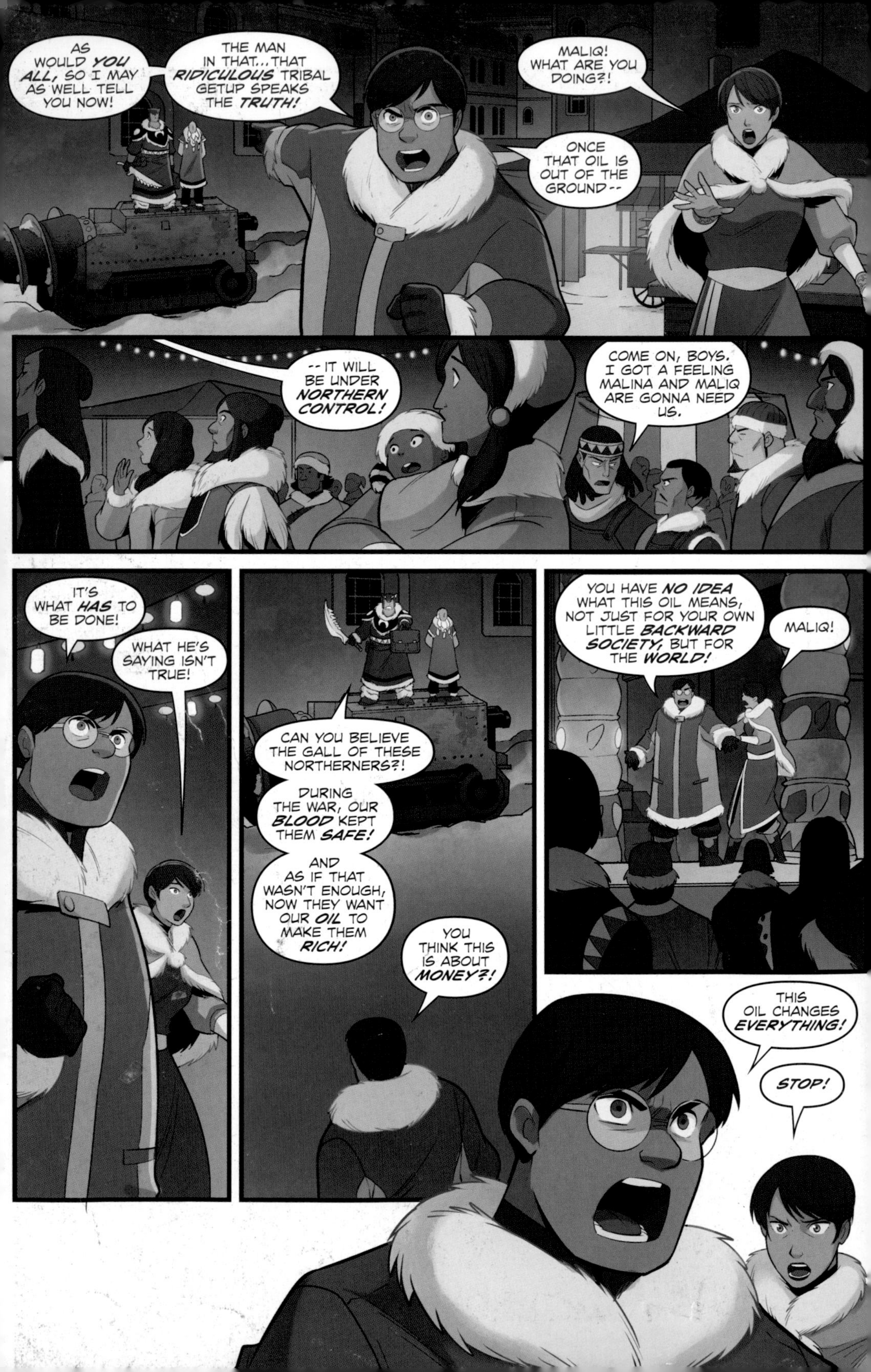
AS WOULD YOU ALL, SO I MAY AS WELL TELL YOU NOW!
THE MAN IN THAT...THAT RIDICULOUS TRIBAL GETUP SPEAKS THE TRUTH!
MALIQ! WHAT ARE YOU DOING?!
ONCE THAT OIL IS OUT OF THE GROUND--
--IT WILL BE UNDER NORTHERN CONTROL!
COME ON, BOYS. I GOT A FEELING MALINA AND MALIQ ARE GONNA NEED US.
IT'S WHAT HAS TO BE DONE!
WHAT HE'S SAYING ISN'T TRUE!
CAN YOU BELIEVE THE GALL OF THESE NORTHERNERS?!
DURING THE WAR, OUR BLOOD KEPT THEM SAFE!
AND AS IF THAT WASN'T ENOUGH, NOW THEY WANT OUR OIL TO MAKE THEM RICH!
YOU THINK THIS IS ABOUT MONEY?!
YOU HAVE NO IDEA WHAT THIS OIL MEANS, NOT JUST FOR YOUR OWN LITTLE BACKWARD SOCIETY, BUT FOR THE WORLD!
MALIQ!
THIS OIL CHANGES EVERYTHING!
STOP!

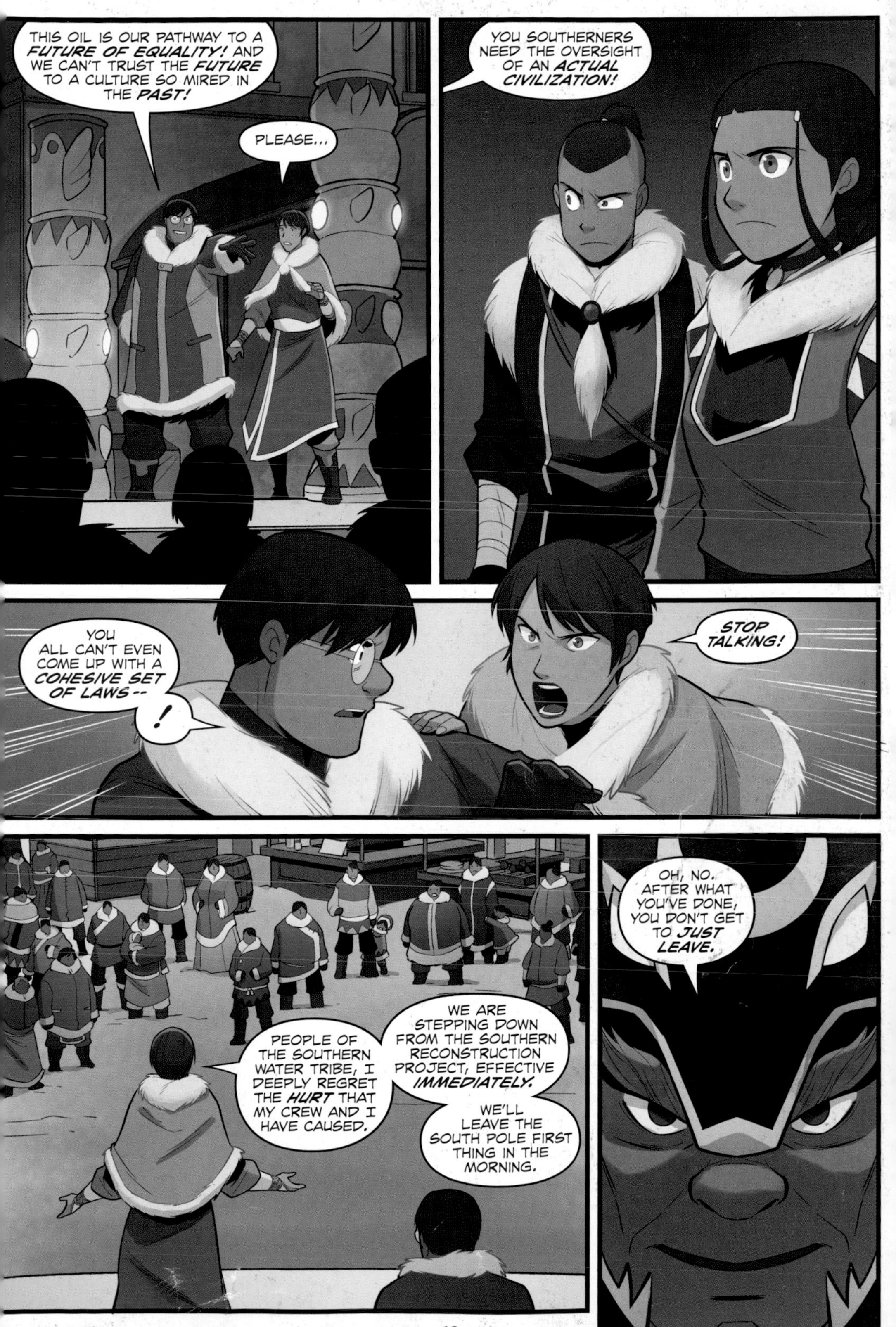

THIS OIL IS OUR PATHWAY TO A FUTURE OF EQUALITY! AND WE CAN'T TRUST THE FUTURE TO A CULTURE SO MIRED IN THE PAST!
PLEASE...
YOU SOUTHERNERS NEED THE OVERSIGHT OF AN ACTUAL CIVILIZATION!
YOU ALL CAN'T EVEN COME UP WITH A COHESIVE SET OF LAWS --
!
STOP TALKING!
PEOPLE OF THE SOUTHERN WATER TRIBE, I DEEPLY REGRET THE HURT THAT MY CREW AND I HAVE CAUSED.
WE ARE STEPPING DOWN FROM THE SOUTHERN RECONSTRUCTION PROJECT, EFFECTIVE IMMEDIATELY.
WE'LL LEAVE THE SOUTH POLE FIRST THING IN THE MORNING.
OH, NO. AFTER WHAT YOU'VE DONE, YOU DON'T GET TO JUST LEAVE.

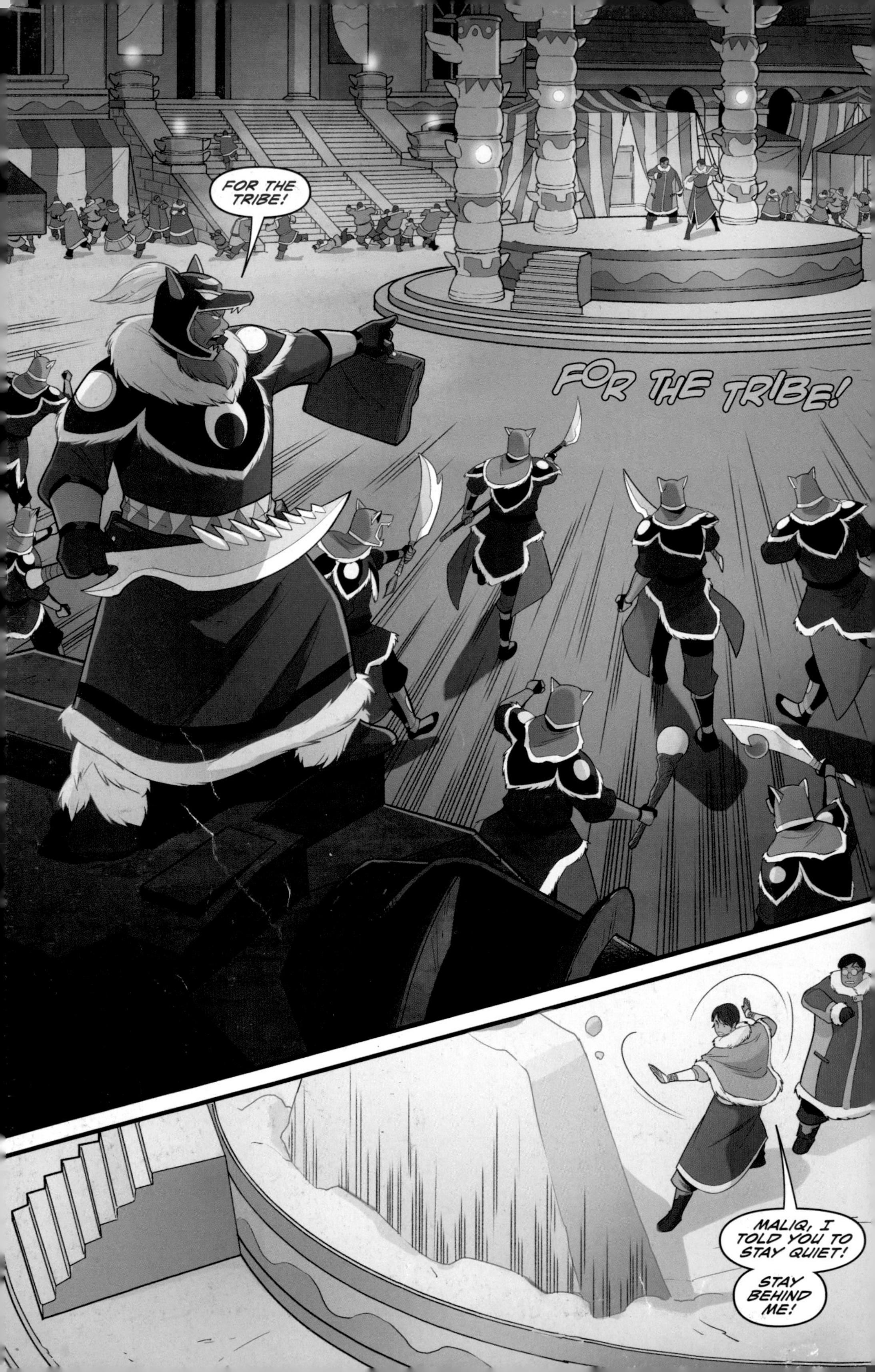
FOR THE TRIBE!
FOR THE TRIBE!
MALIQ, I TOLD YOU TO STAY QUIET!
STAY BEHIND ME!

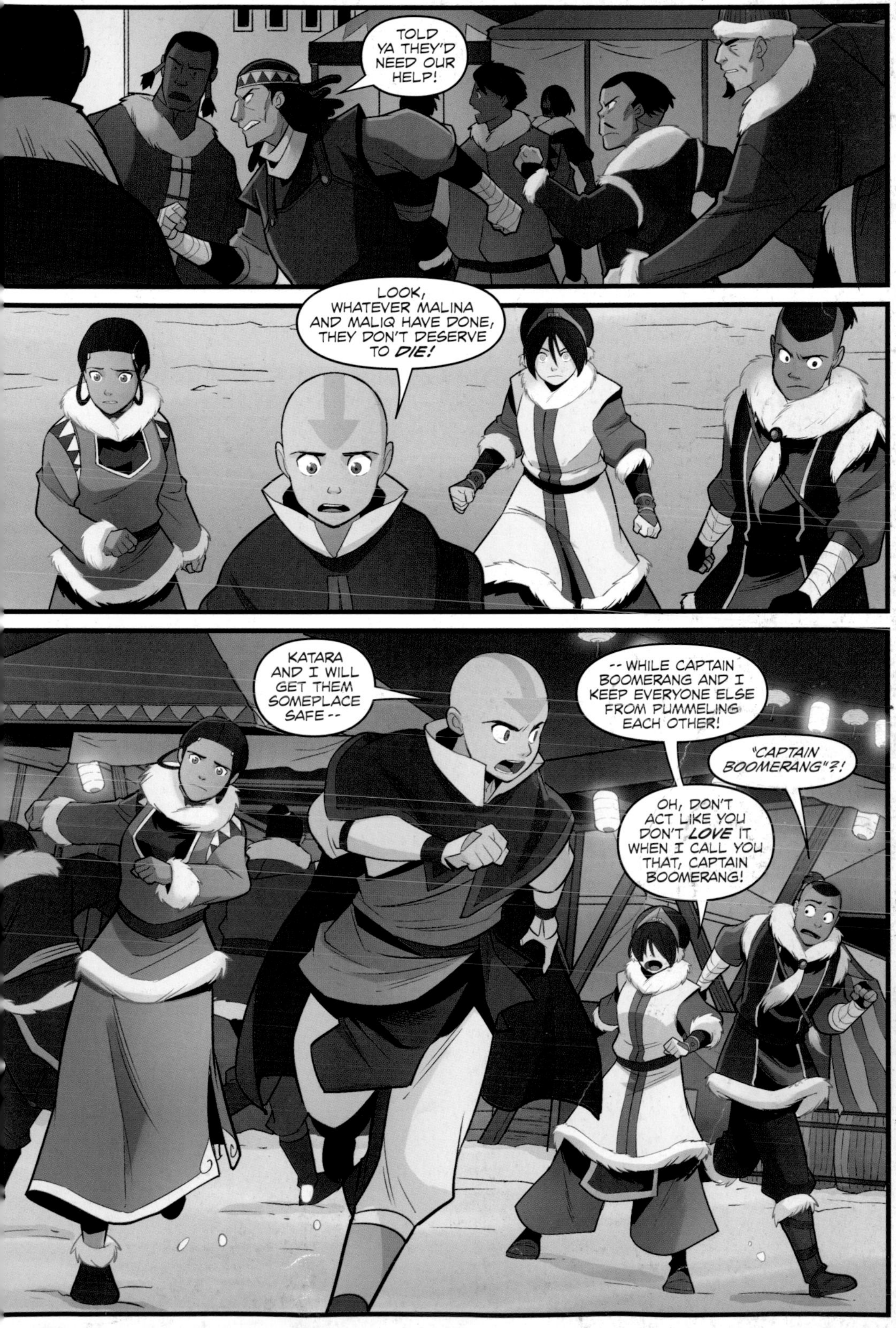
TOLD YA THEY'D NEED OUR HELP!
LOOK, WHATEVER MALINA AND MALIQ HAVE DONE, THEY DON'T DESERVE TO *DIE!*
KATARA AND I WILL GET THEM SOMEPLACE SAFE--
--WHILE CAPTAIN BOOMERANG AND I KEEP EVERYONE ELSE FROM PUMMELING EACH OTHER!
"CAPTAIN BOOMERANG"?!
OH, DON'T ACT LIKE YOU DON'T *LOVE* IT WHEN I CALL YOU THAT, CAPTAIN BOOMERANG!

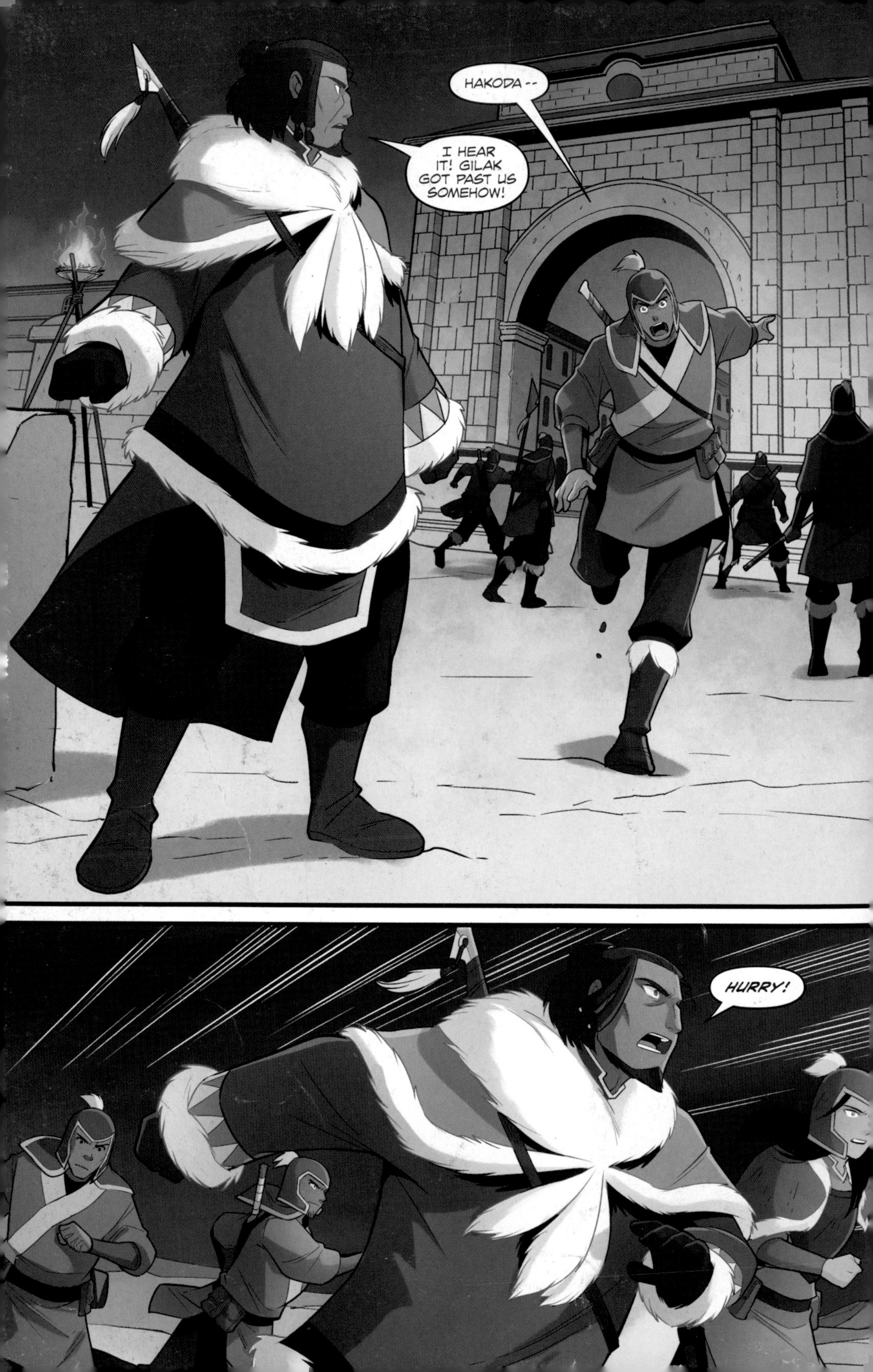
HAKODA --
I HEAR IT! GILAK GOT PAST US SOMEHOW!
HURRY!

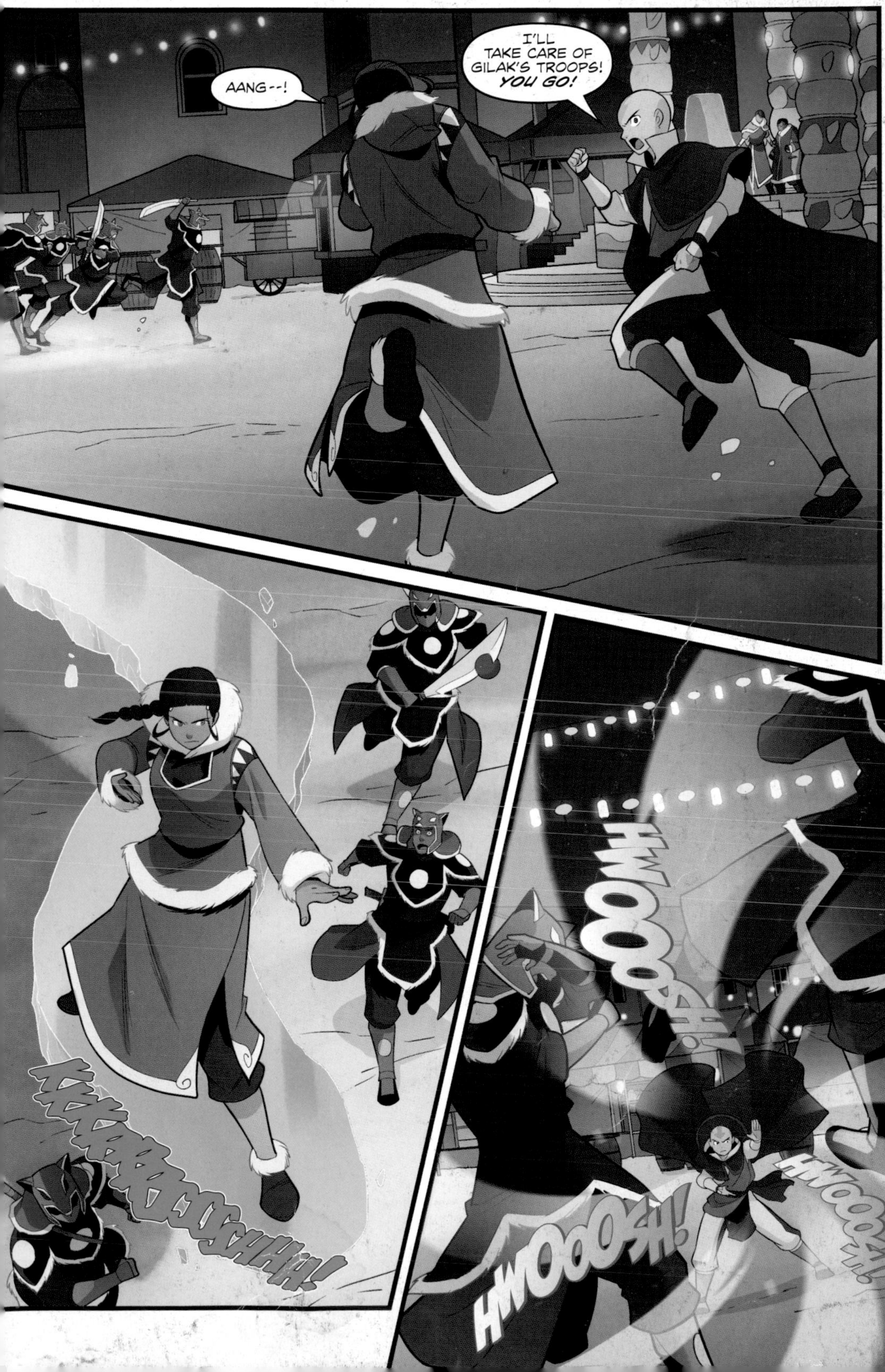

AANG--!
I'LL TAKE CARE OF GILAK'S TROOPS! YOU GO!
KKKKRRROOSCHHH!
HWOOOSH!
HWOOOSH!
HWOOOSH!

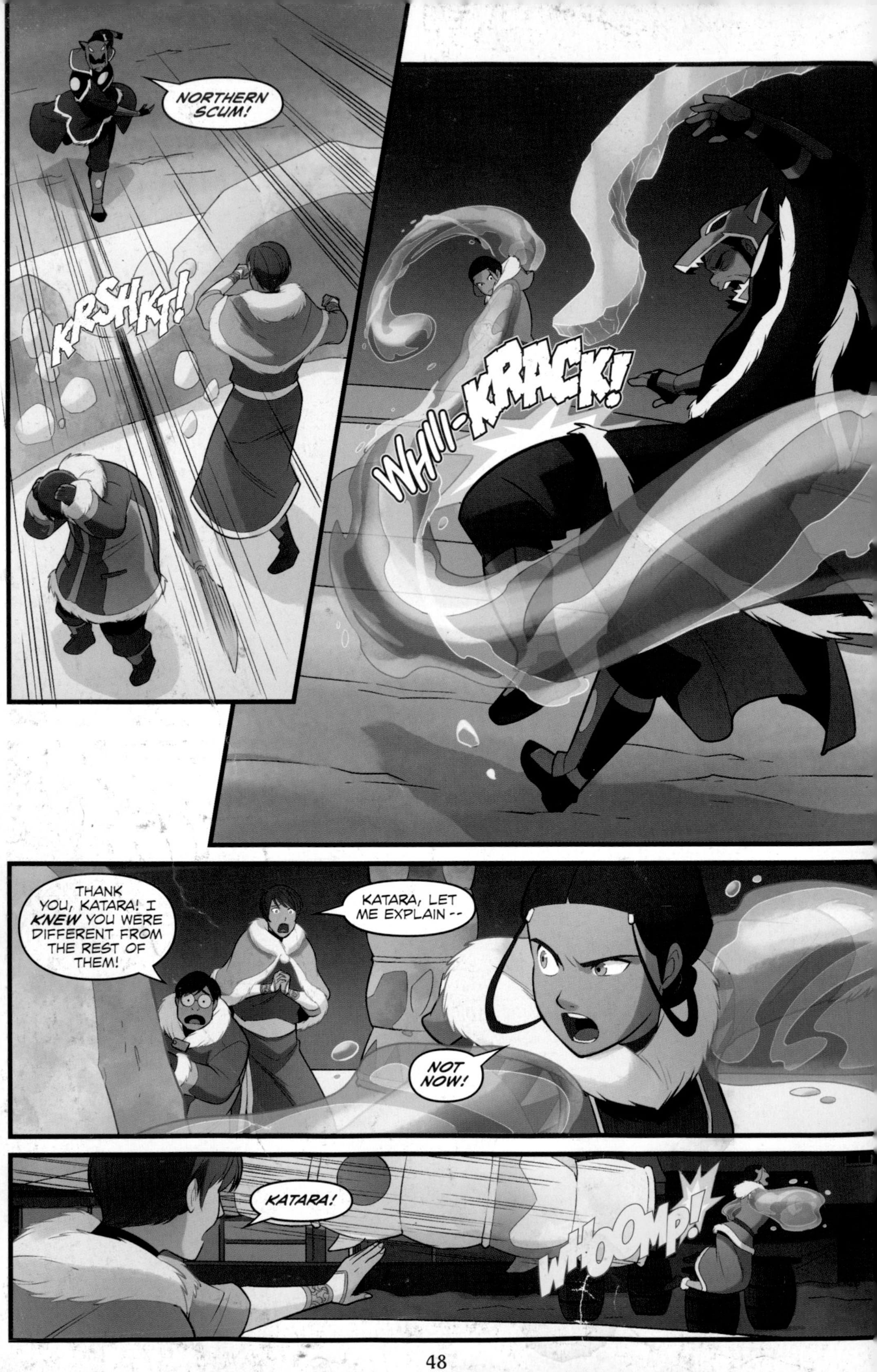
NORTHERN SCUM!
KRSHKT!
WHIII-KRACK!
THANK YOU, KATARA! I KNEW YOU WERE DIFFERENT FROM THE REST OF THEM!
KATARA, LET ME EXPLAIN --
NOT NOW!
KATARA!
WHOOMP!

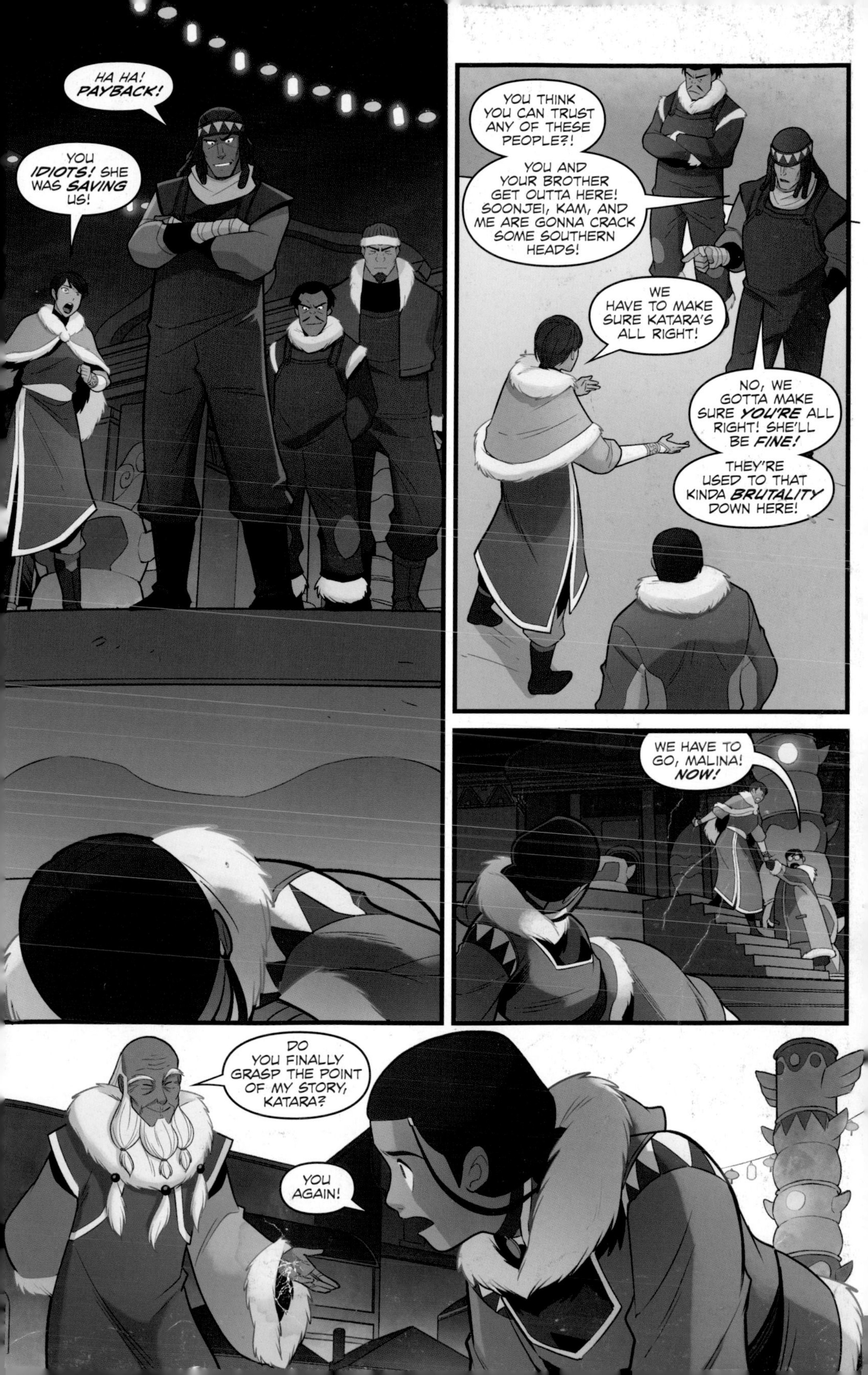
HA HA! PAYBACK!
YOU IDIOTS! SHE WAS SAVING US!
YOU THINK YOU CAN TRUST ANY OF THESE PEOPLE?!
YOU AND YOUR BROTHER GET OUTTA HERE! SOONJEI, KAM, AND ME ARE GONNA CRACK SOME SOUTHERN HEADS!
WE HAVE TO MAKE SURE KATARA'S ALL RIGHT!
NO, WE GOTTA MAKE SURE YOU'RE ALL RIGHT! SHE'LL BE FINE!
THEY'RE USED TO THAT KINDA BRUTALITY DOWN HERE!
WE HAVE TO GO, MALINA! NOW!
DO YOU FINALLY GRASP THE POINT OF MY STORY, KATARA?
YOU AGAIN!

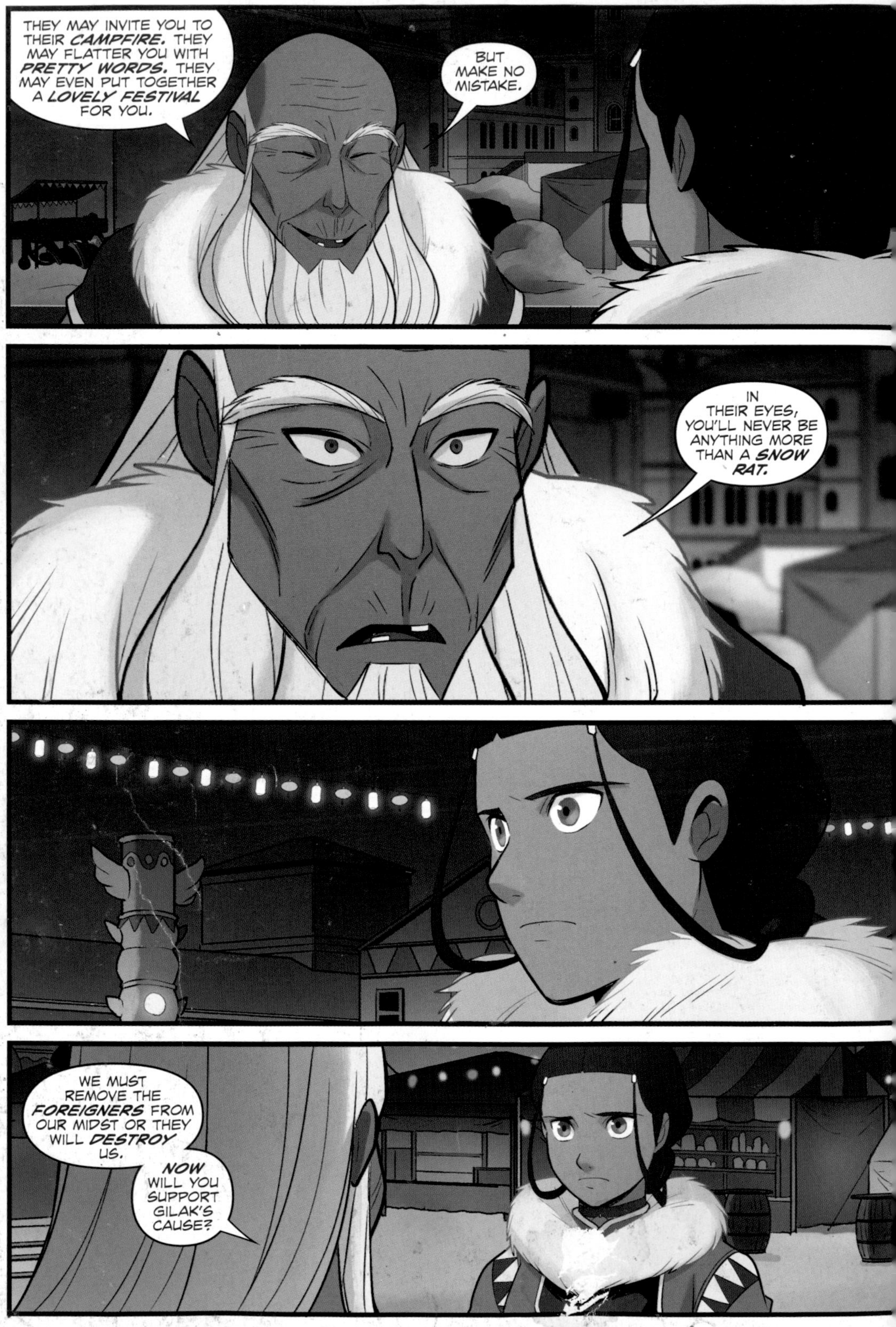
THEY MAY INVITE YOU TO THEIR *CAMPFIRE.* THEY MAY FLATTER YOU WITH *PRETTY WORDS.* THEY MAY EVEN PUT TOGETHER A *LOVELY FESTIVAL* FOR YOU.
BUT MAKE NO MISTAKE.
IN THEIR EYES, YOU'LL NEVER BE ANYTHING MORE THAN A *SNOW RAT.*
WE MUST REMOVE THE *FOREIGNERS* FROM OUR MIDST OR THEY WILL *DESTROY* US.
NOW WILL YOU SUPPORT GILAK'S CAUSE?

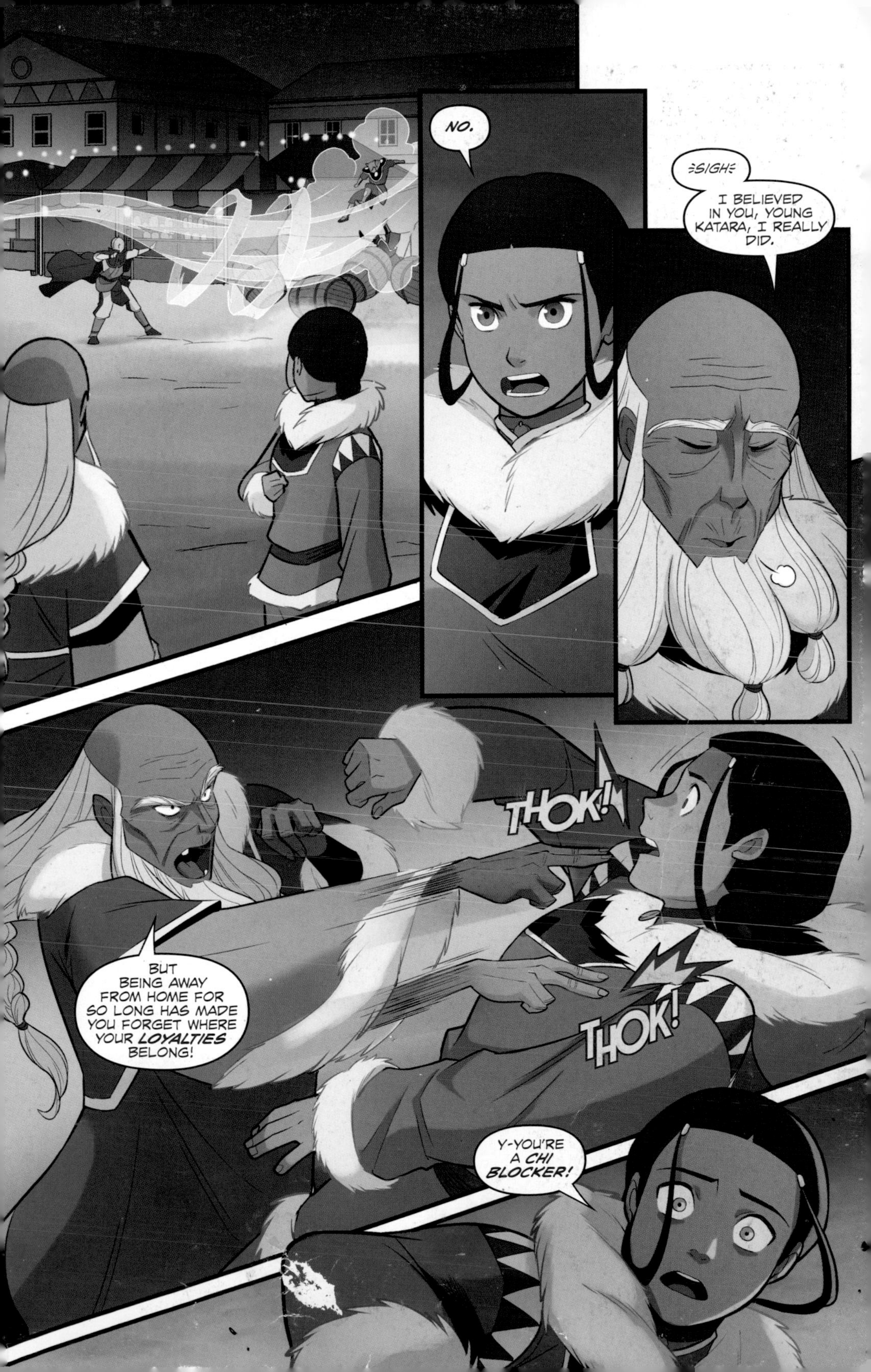
NO.
SIGH
I BELIEVED IN YOU, YOUNG KATARA, I REALLY DID.
THOK!
BUT BEING AWAY FROM HOME FOR SO LONG HAS MADE YOU FORGET WHERE YOUR LOYALTIES BELONG!
THOK!
Y-YOU'RE A CHI BLOCKER!

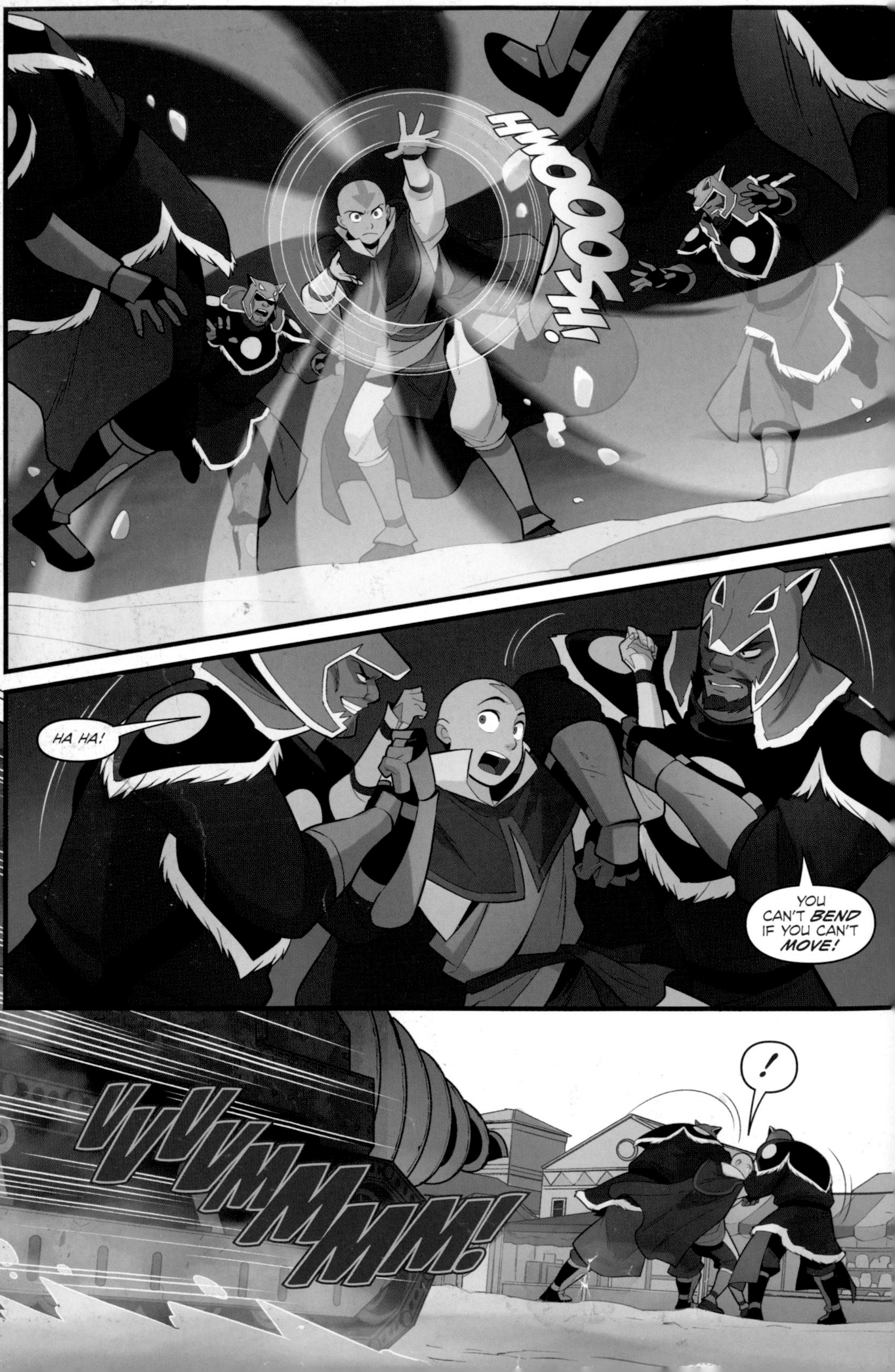
HWOOOSH!
HA HA!
YOU CAN'T BEND IF YOU CAN'T MOVE!
!
VV-VMMMMM!

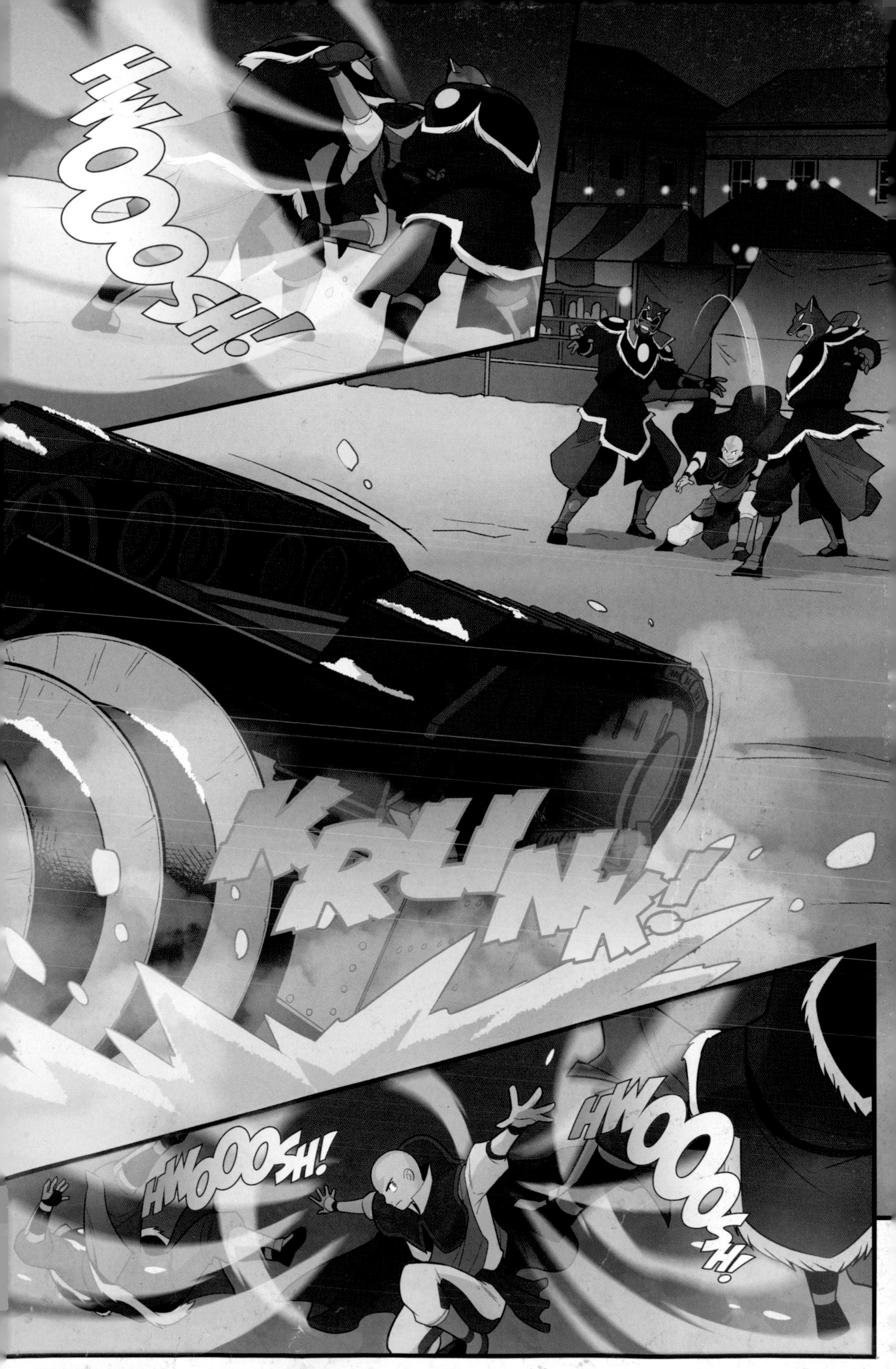
HWOOOSH!
KRUNK!
HWOOOSH!
HWOOOOSH!

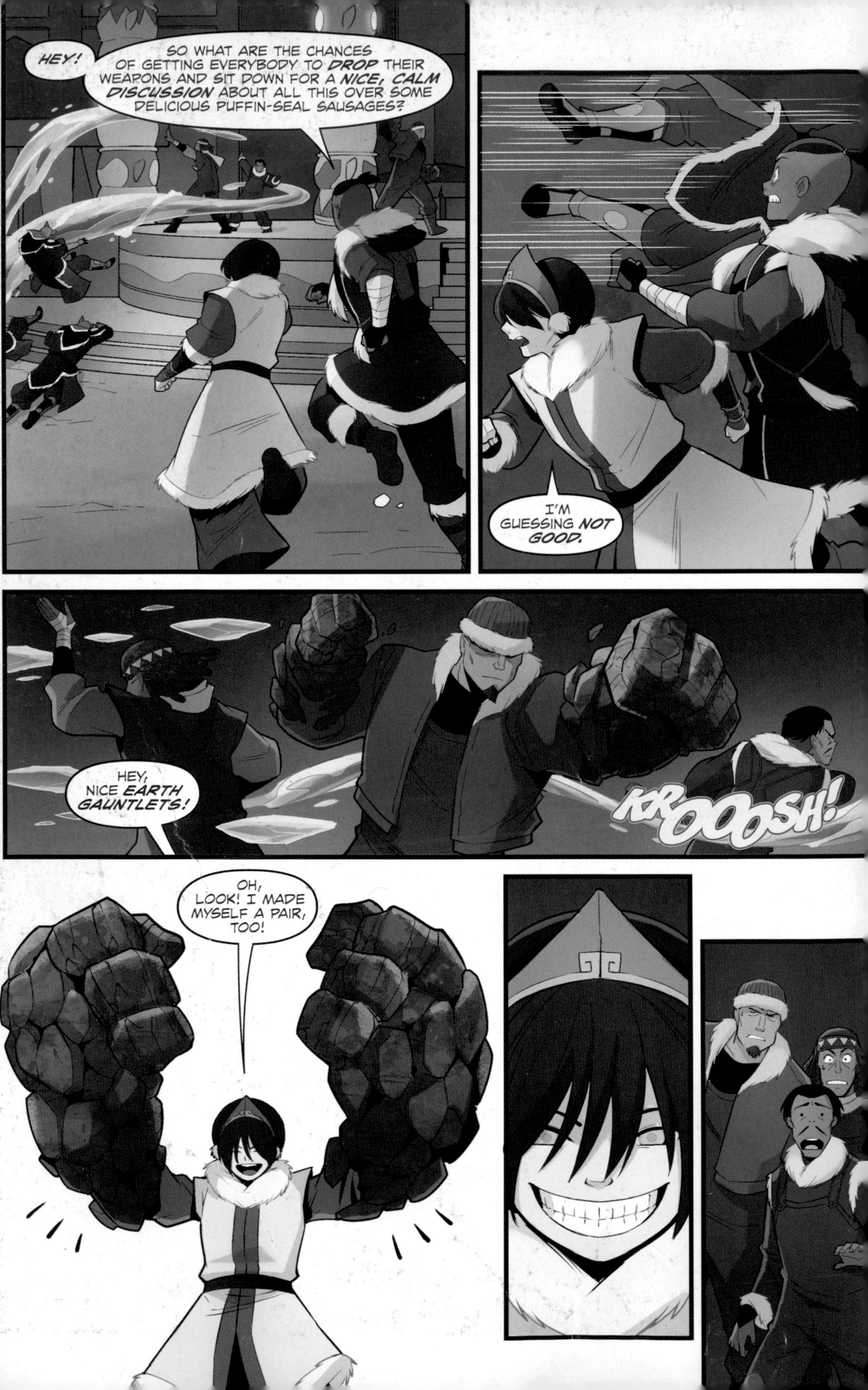
HEY!
SO WHAT ARE THE CHANCES OF GETTING EVERYBODY TO DROP THEIR WEAPONS AND SIT DOWN FOR A NICE, CALM DISCUSSION ABOUT ALL THIS OVER SOME DELICIOUS PUFFIN-SEAL SAUSAGES?
I'M GUESSING NOT GOOD.
HEY, NICE EARTH GAUNTLETS!
KROOOOSH!
OH, LOOK! I MADE MYSELF A PAIR, TOO!

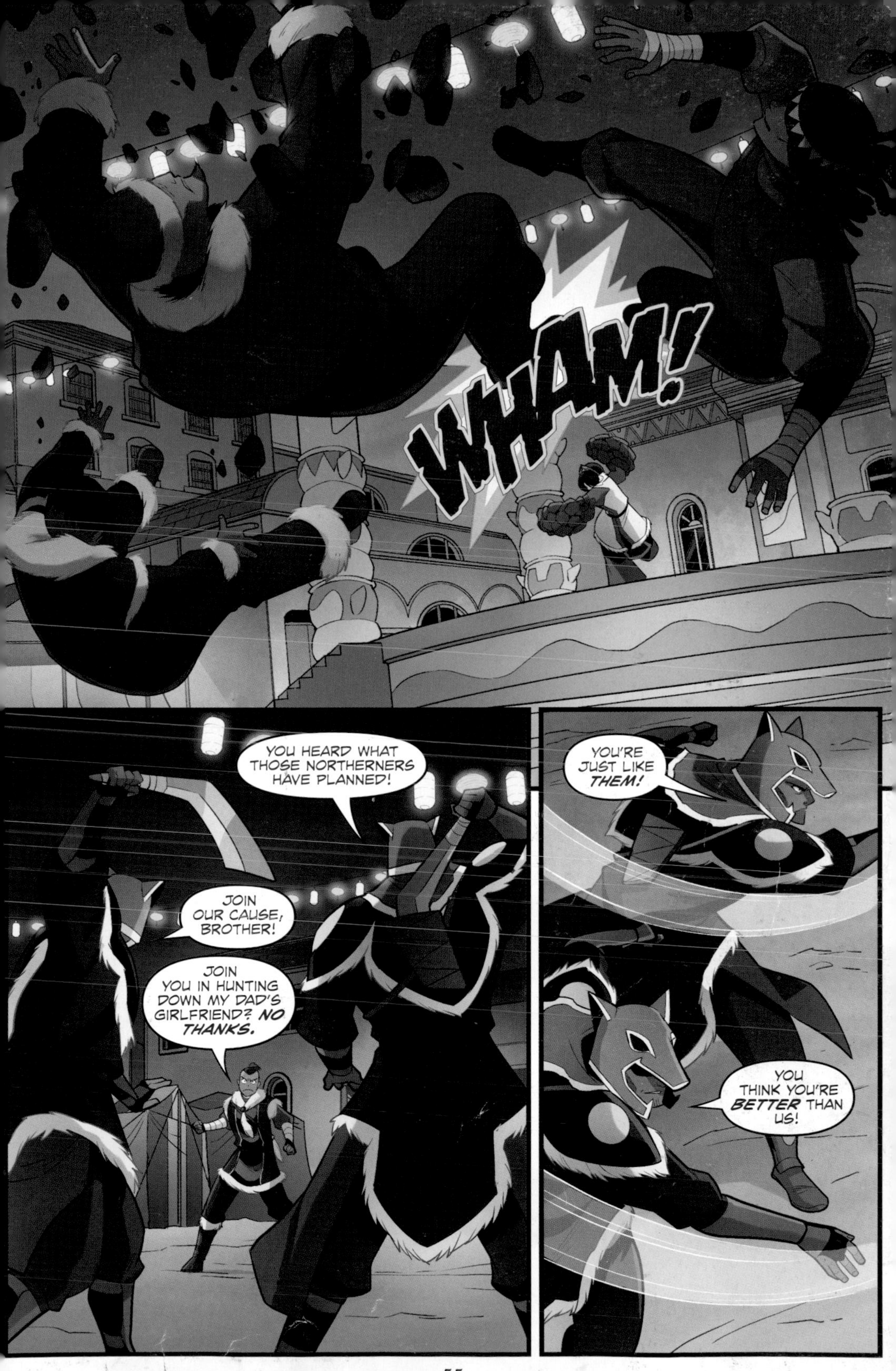
WHAM!
YOU HEARD WHAT THOSE NORTHERNERS HAVE PLANNED!
JOIN OUR CAUSE, BROTHER!
JOIN YOU IN HUNTING DOWN MY DAD'S GIRLFRIEND? NO THANKS.
YOU'RE JUST LIKE THEM!
YOU THINK YOU'RE BETTER THAN US!

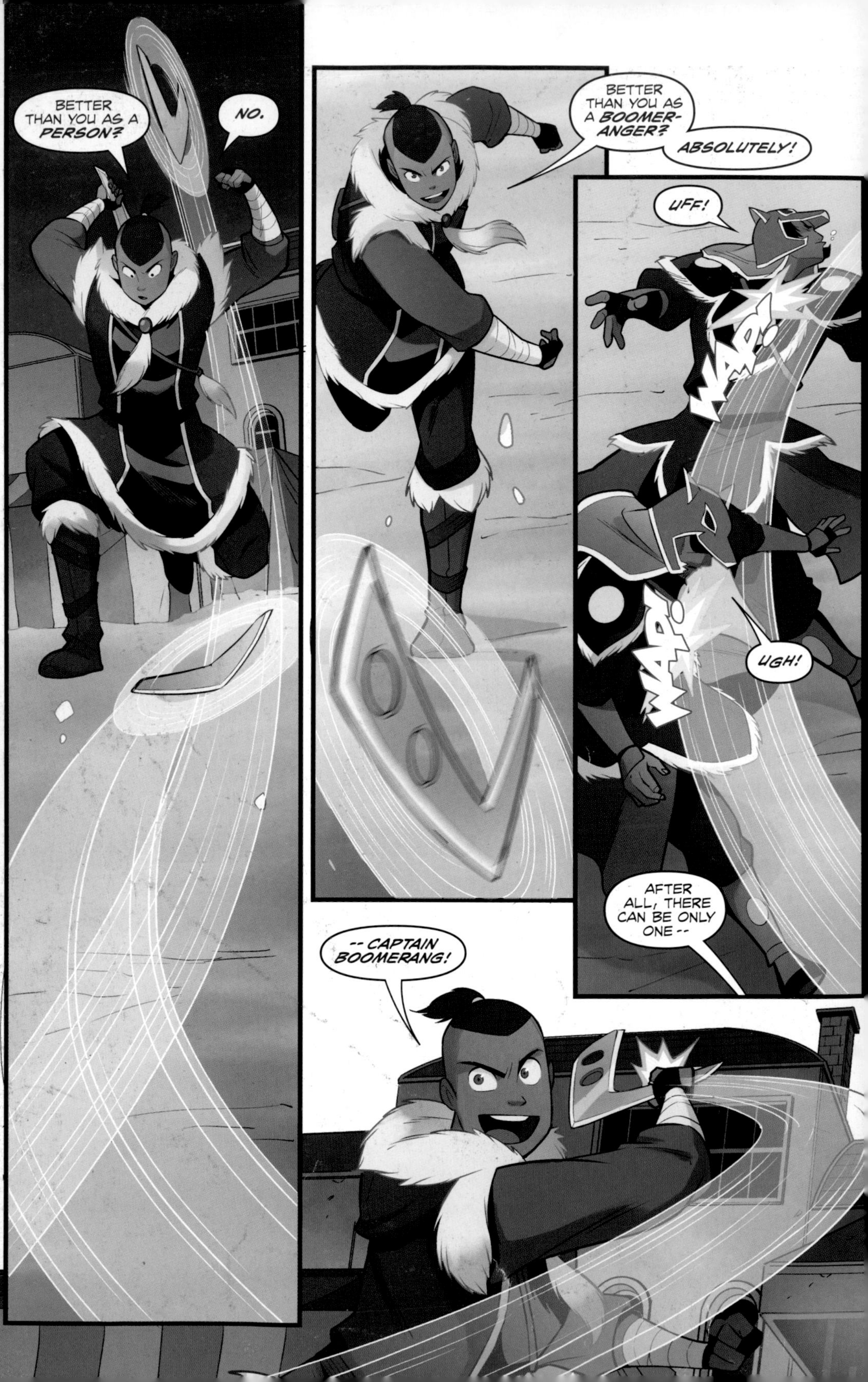
BETTER THAN YOU AS A PERSON?
NO.
BETTER THAN YOU AS A BOOMER-ANGER?
ABSOLUTELY!
UFF!
WAP!
WAP!
UGH!
AFTER ALL, THERE CAN BE ONLY ONE --
-- CAPTAIN BOOMERANG!

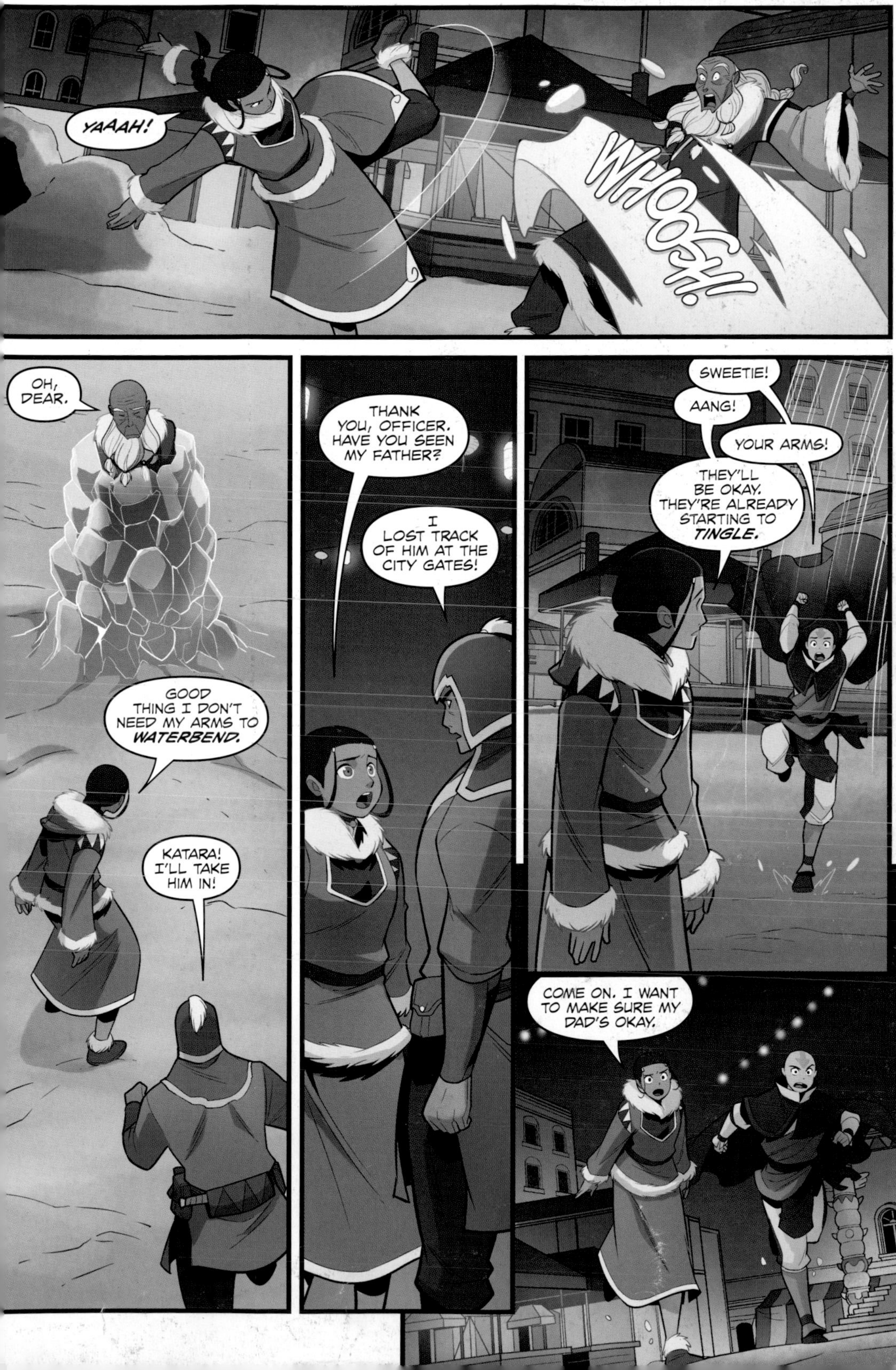
YAAAH!
WHOOSH!
OH, DEAR.
GOOD THING I DON'T NEED MY ARMS TO WATERBEND.
KATARA! I'LL TAKE HIM IN!
THANK YOU, OFFICER. HAVE YOU SEEN MY FATHER?
I LOST TRACK OF HIM AT THE CITY GATES!
SWEETIE!
AANG!
YOUR ARMS!
THEY'LL BE OKAY. THEY'RE ALREADY STARTING TO TINGLE.
COME ON. I WANT TO MAKE SURE MY DAD'S OKAY.

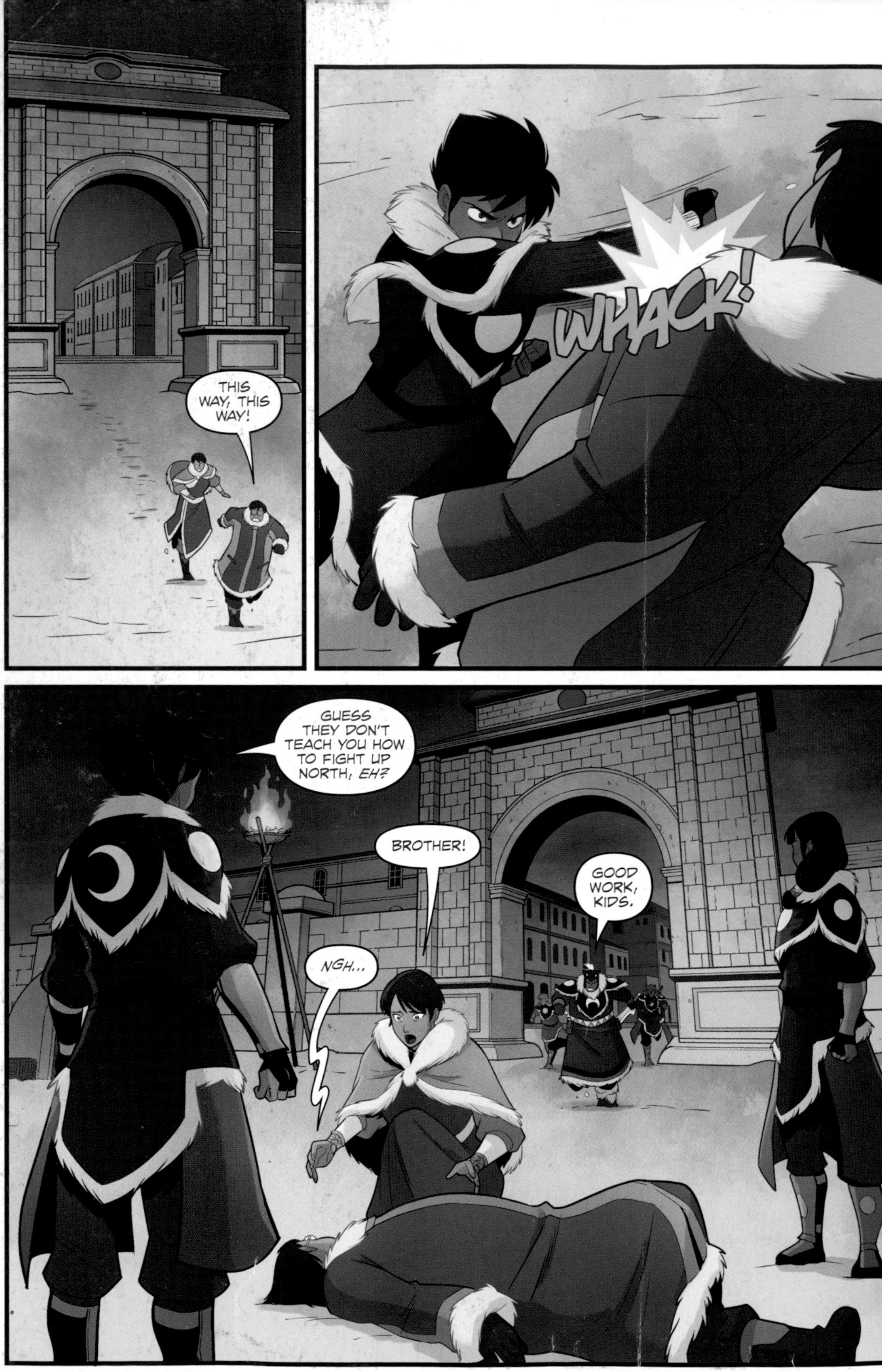
THIS WAY, THIS WAY!
WHACK!
GUESS THEY DON'T TEACH YOU HOW TO FIGHT UP NORTH, *EH?*
BROTHER!
GOOD WORK, KIDS.
NGH...

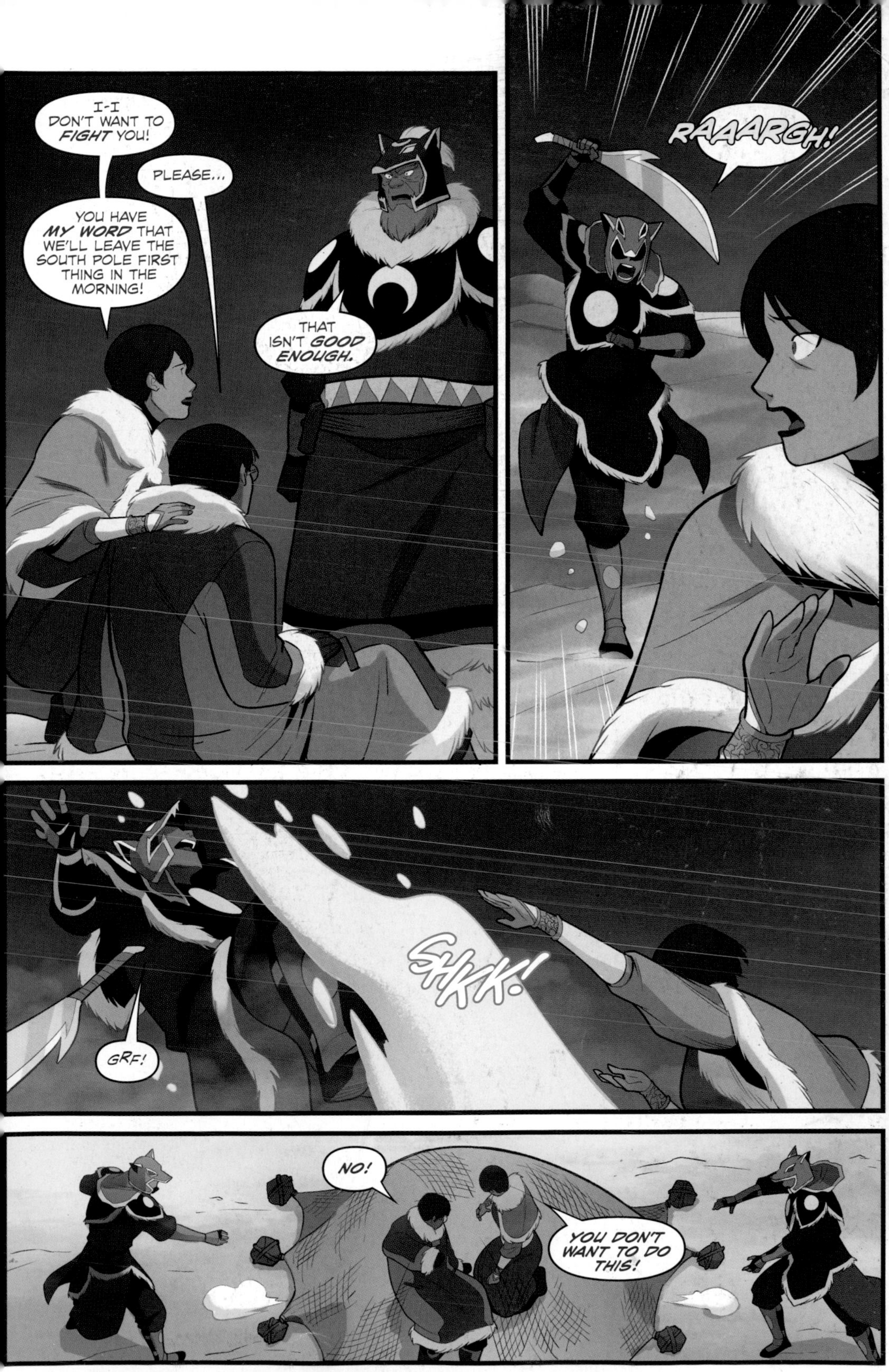
I-I DON'T WANT TO FIGHT YOU!
PLEASE...
YOU HAVE MY WORD THAT WE'LL LEAVE THE SOUTH POLE FIRST THING IN THE MORNING!
THAT ISN'T GOOD ENOUGH.
RAAARGH!
SHKK!
GRF!
NO!
YOU DON'T WANT TO DO THIS!

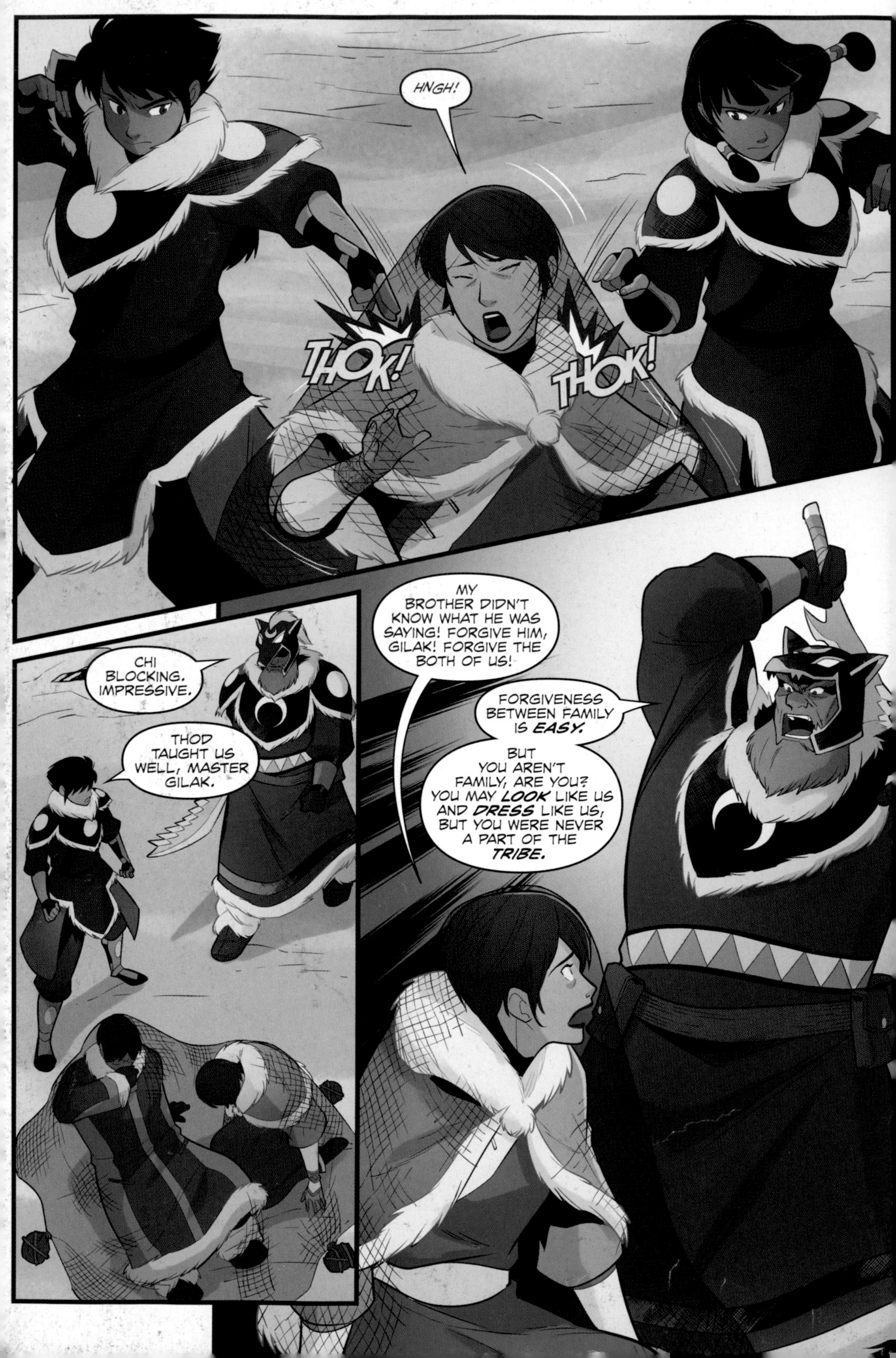
HNGH!
THOK!
THOK!
CHI BLOCKING. IMPRESSIVE.
THOD TAUGHT US WELL, MASTER GILAK.
MY BROTHER DIDN'T KNOW WHAT HE WAS SAYING! FORGIVE HIM, GILAK! FORGIVE THE BOTH OF US!
FORGIVENESS BETWEEN FAMILY IS EASY.
BUT YOU AREN'T FAMILY, ARE YOU? YOU MAY LOOK LIKE US AND DRESS LIKE US, BUT YOU WERE NEVER A PART OF THE TRIBE.

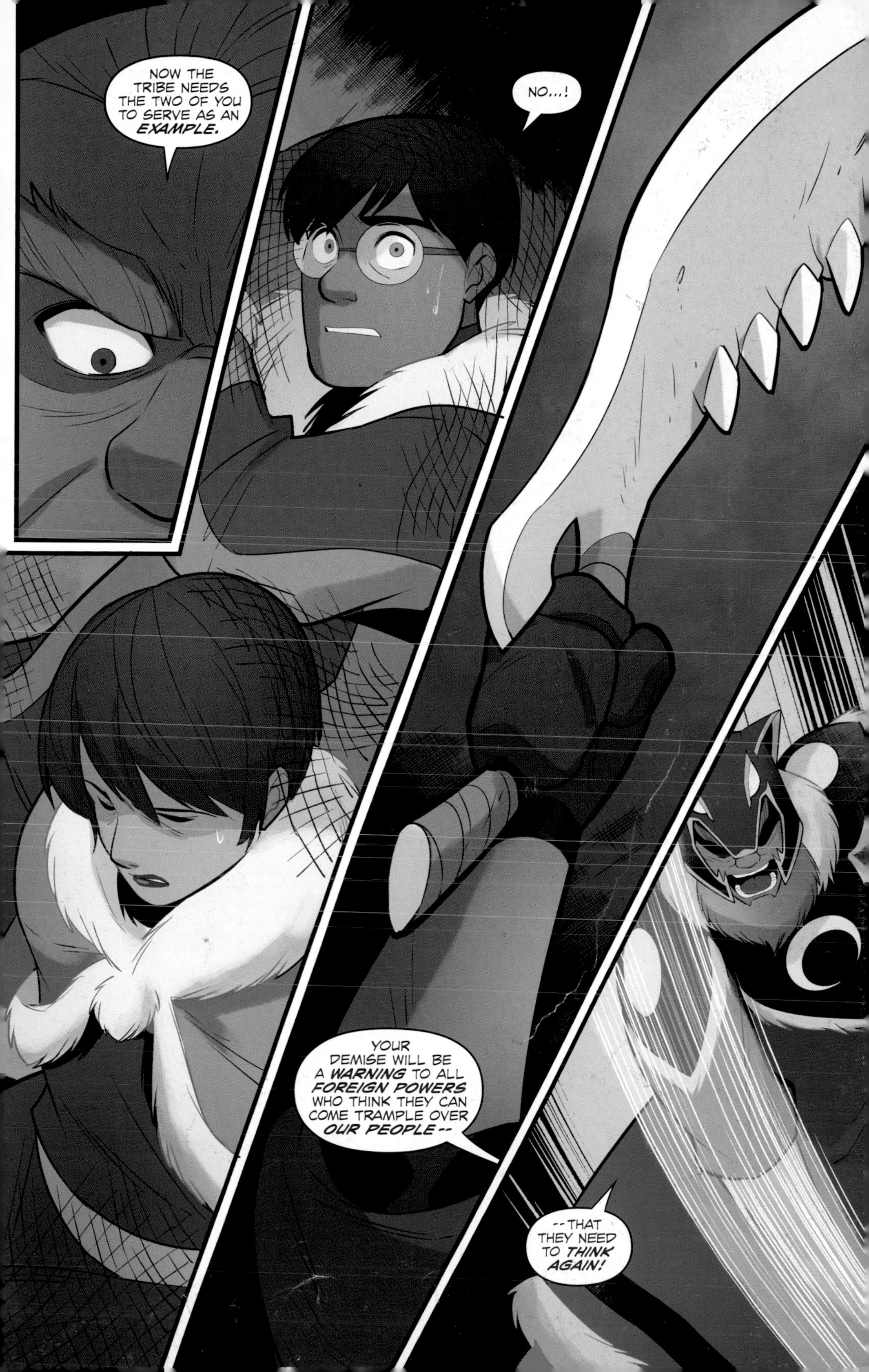
NOW THE TRIBE NEEDS THE TWO OF YOU TO SERVE AS AN EXAMPLE.
NO...!
YOUR DEMISE WILL BE A WARNING TO ALL FOREIGN POWERS WHO THINK THEY CAN COME TRAMPLE OVER OUR PEOPLE--
--THAT THEY NEED TO THINK AGAIN!

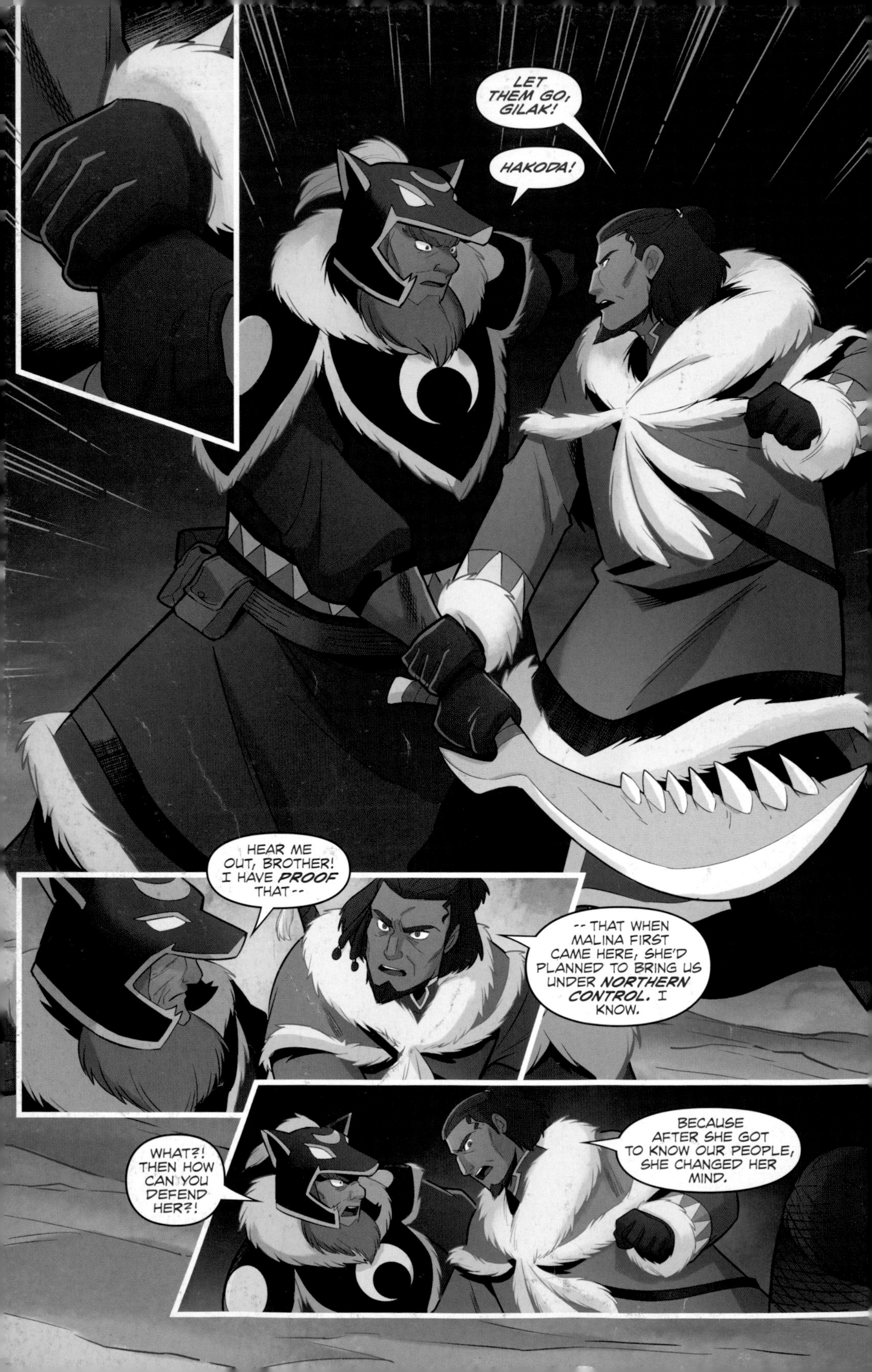
LET THEM GO, GILAK!
HAKODA!
HEAR ME OUT, BROTHER! I HAVE PROOF THAT--
--THAT WHEN MALINA FIRST CAME HERE, SHE'D PLANNED TO BRING US UNDER NORTHERN CONTROL. I KNOW.
WHAT?! THEN HOW CAN YOU DEFEND HER?!
BECAUSE AFTER SHE GOT TO KNOW OUR PEOPLE, SHE CHANGED HER MIND.

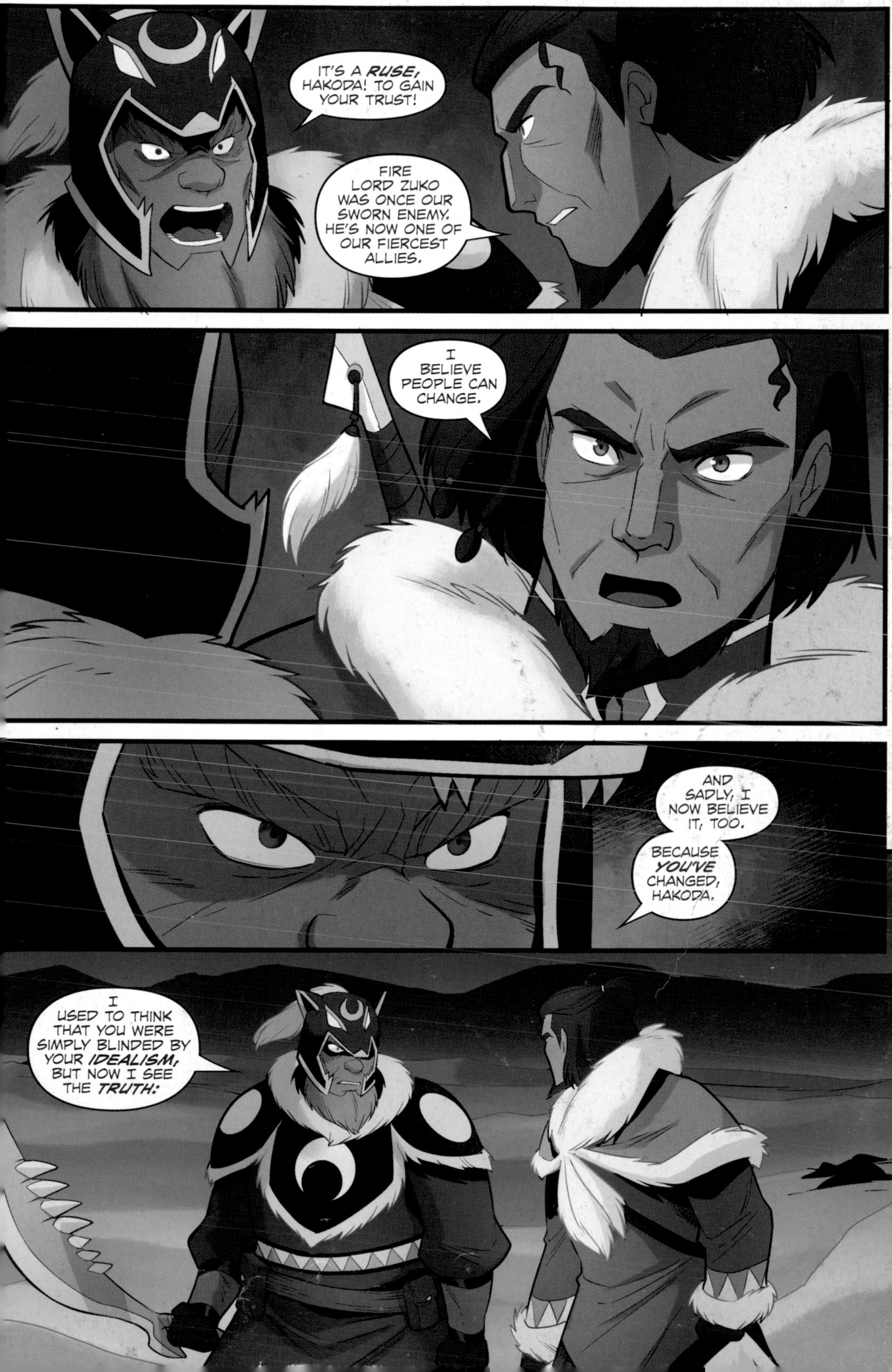
IT'S A RUSE, HAKODA! TO GAIN YOUR TRUST!
FIRE LORD ZUKO WAS ONCE OUR SWORN ENEMY. HE'S NOW ONE OF OUR FIERCEST ALLIES.
I BELIEVE PEOPLE CAN CHANGE.
AND SADLY, I NOW BELIEVE IT, TOO.
BECAUSE YOU'VE CHANGED, HAKODA.
I USED TO THINK THAT YOU WERE SIMPLY BLINDED BY YOUR IDEALISM, BUT NOW I SEE THE TRUTH:

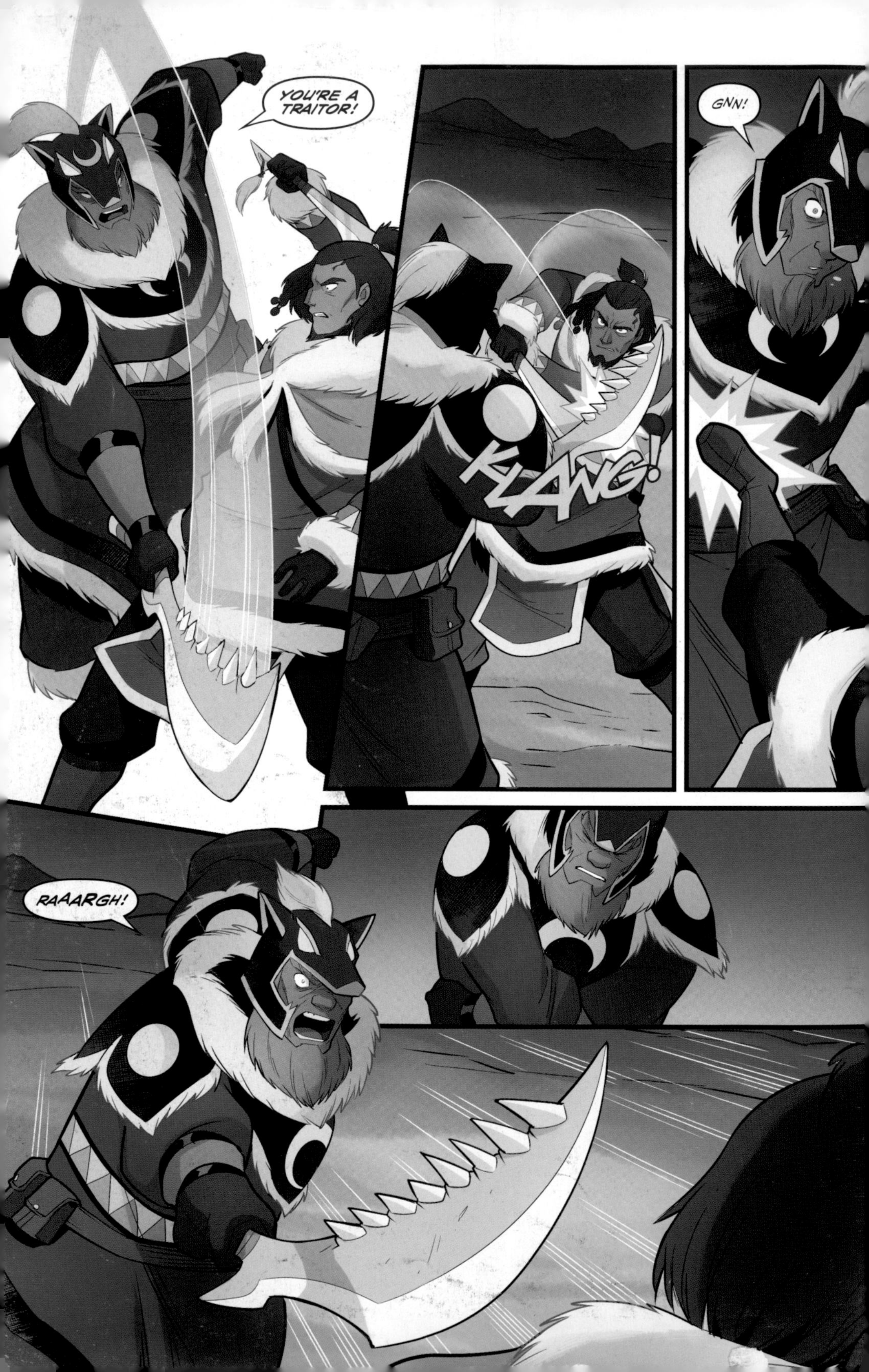
YOU'RE A TRAITOR!
KLANG!
GNN!
RAAARGH!

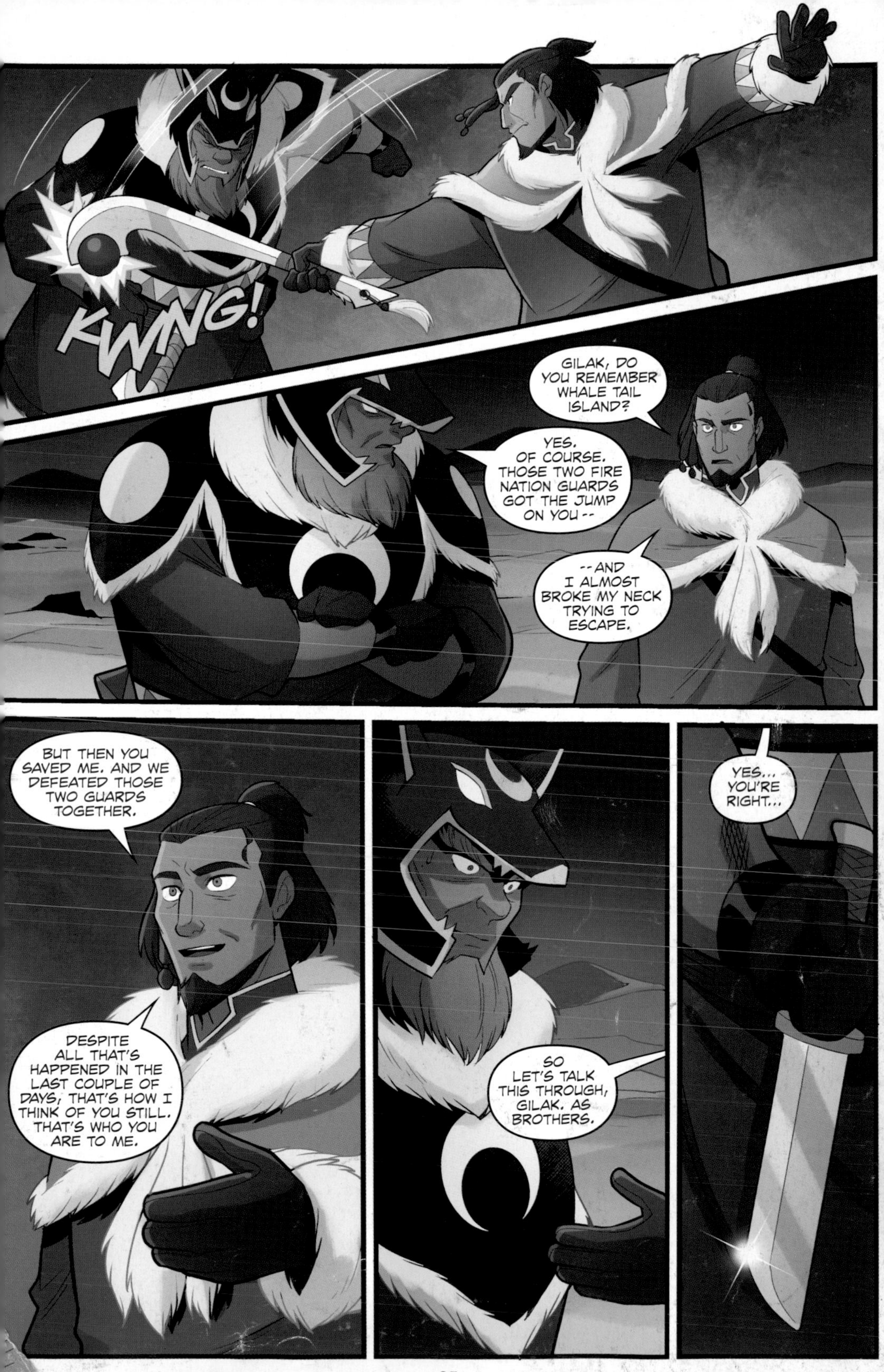
KWNG!
GILAK, DO YOU REMEMBER WHALE TAIL ISLAND?
YES. OF COURSE. THOSE TWO FIRE NATION GUARDS GOT THE JUMP ON YOU --
-- AND I ALMOST BROKE MY NECK TRYING TO ESCAPE.
BUT THEN YOU SAVED ME. AND WE DEFEATED THOSE TWO GUARDS TOGETHER.
DESPITE ALL THAT'S HAPPENED IN THE LAST COUPLE OF DAYS, THAT'S HOW I THINK OF YOU STILL. THAT'S WHO YOU ARE TO ME.
SO LET'S TALK THIS THROUGH, GILAK. AS BROTHERS.
YES... YOU'RE RIGHT...

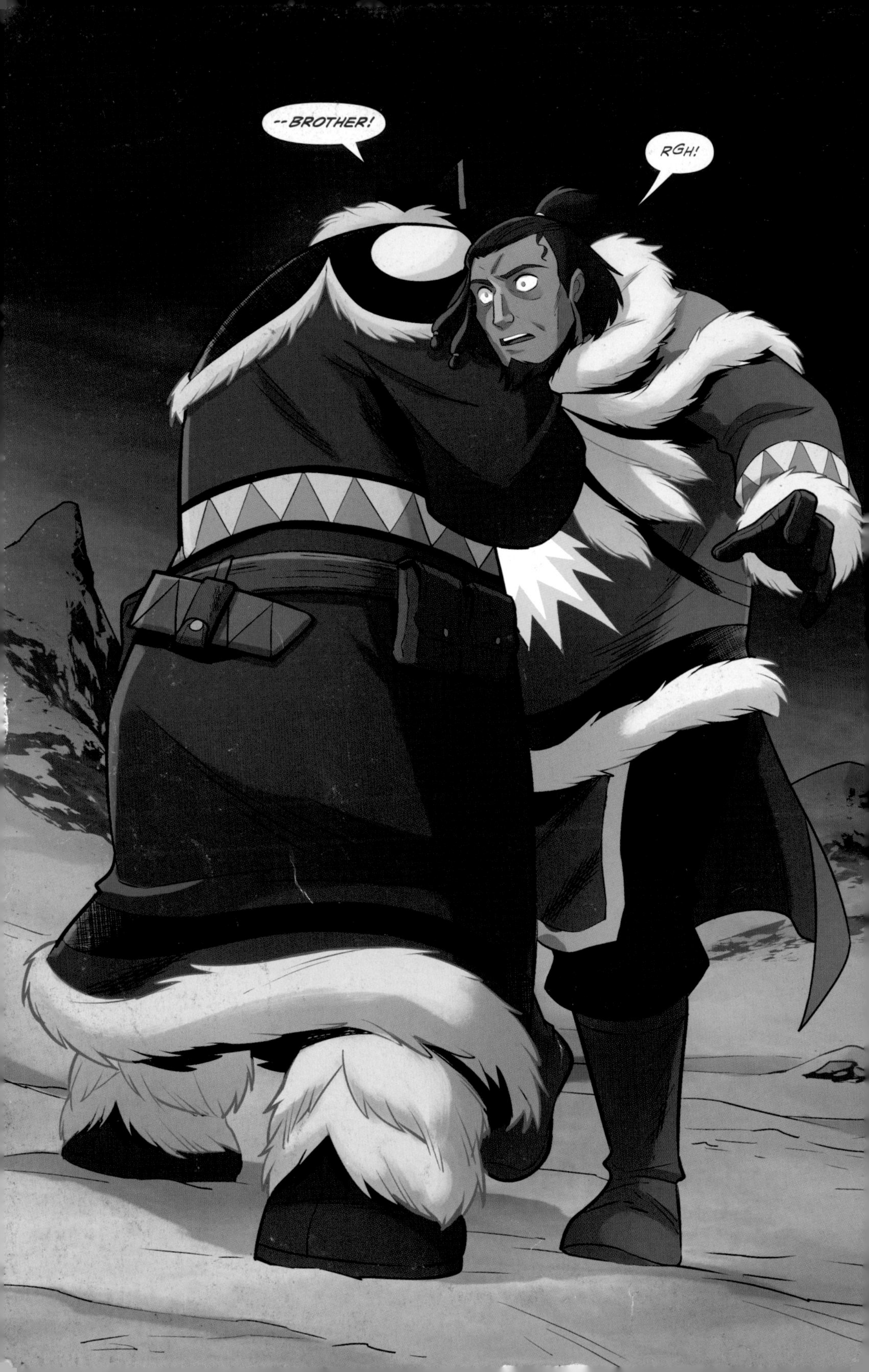
--BROTHER!
RGH!

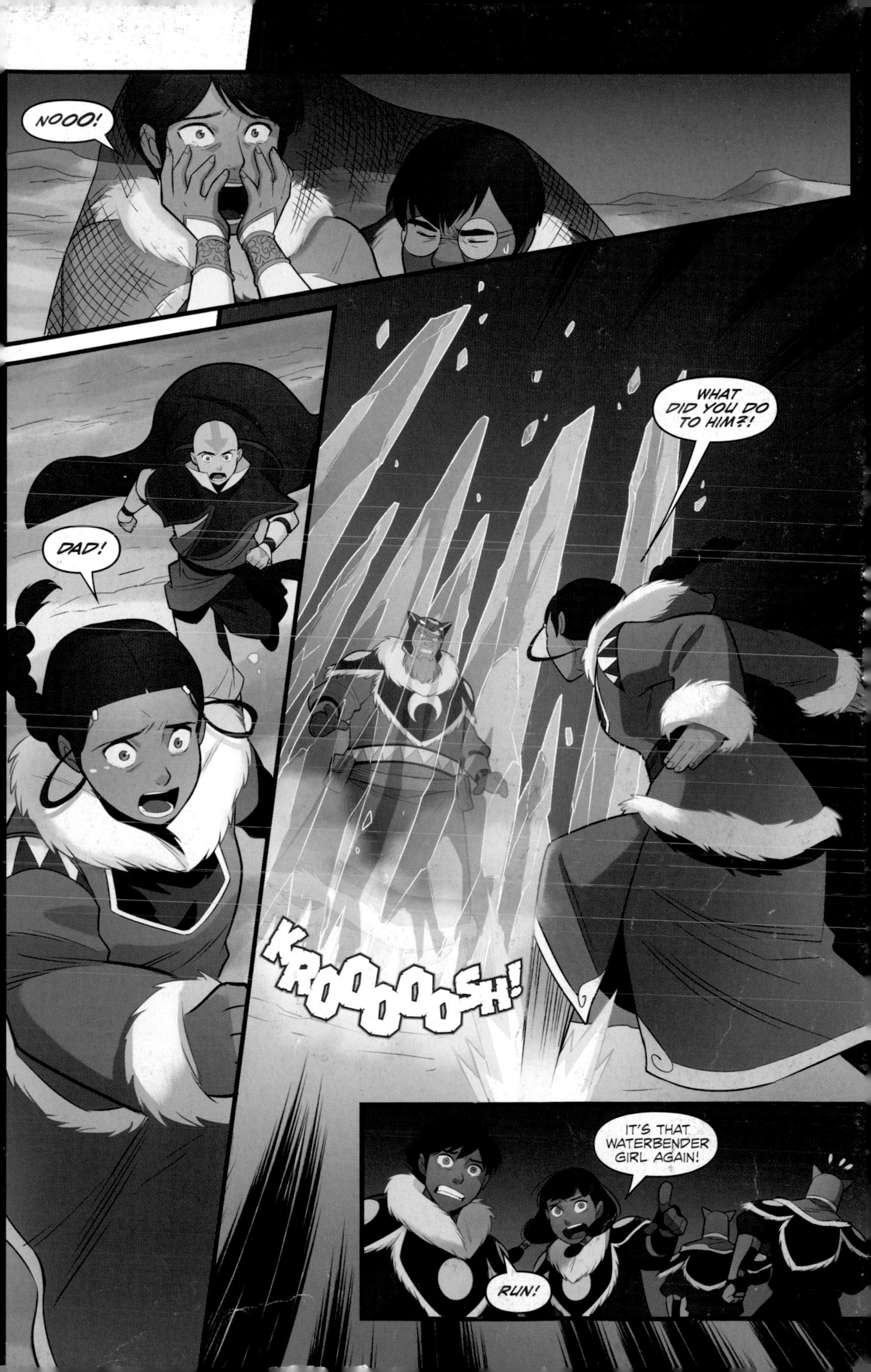
NOOO!
DAD!
WHAT DID YOU DO TO HIM?!
KROOOOOOSH!
IT'S THAT WATERBENDER GIRL AGAIN!
RUN!

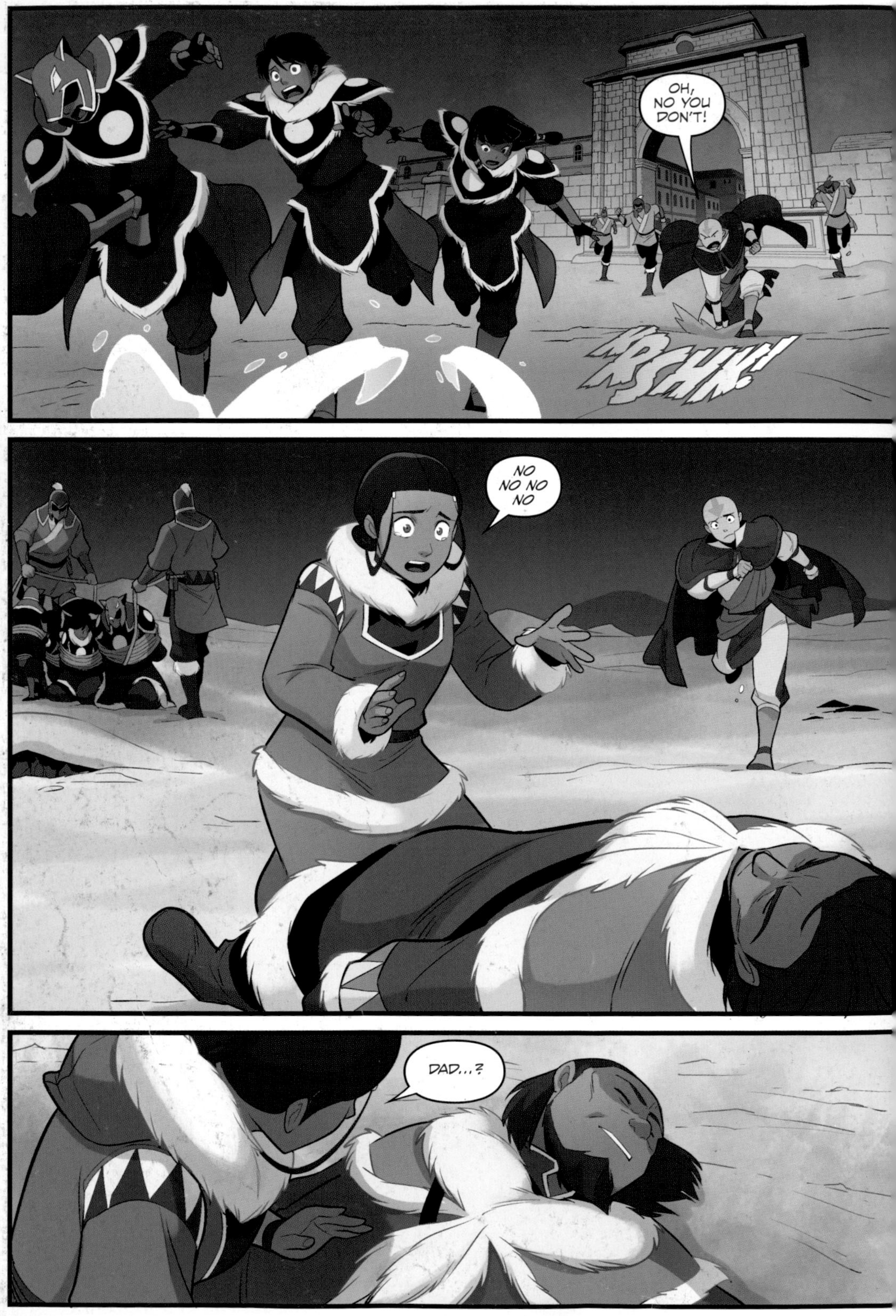
OH, NO YOU DON'T!
KRSHK!!
NO NO NO NO NO
DAD...?

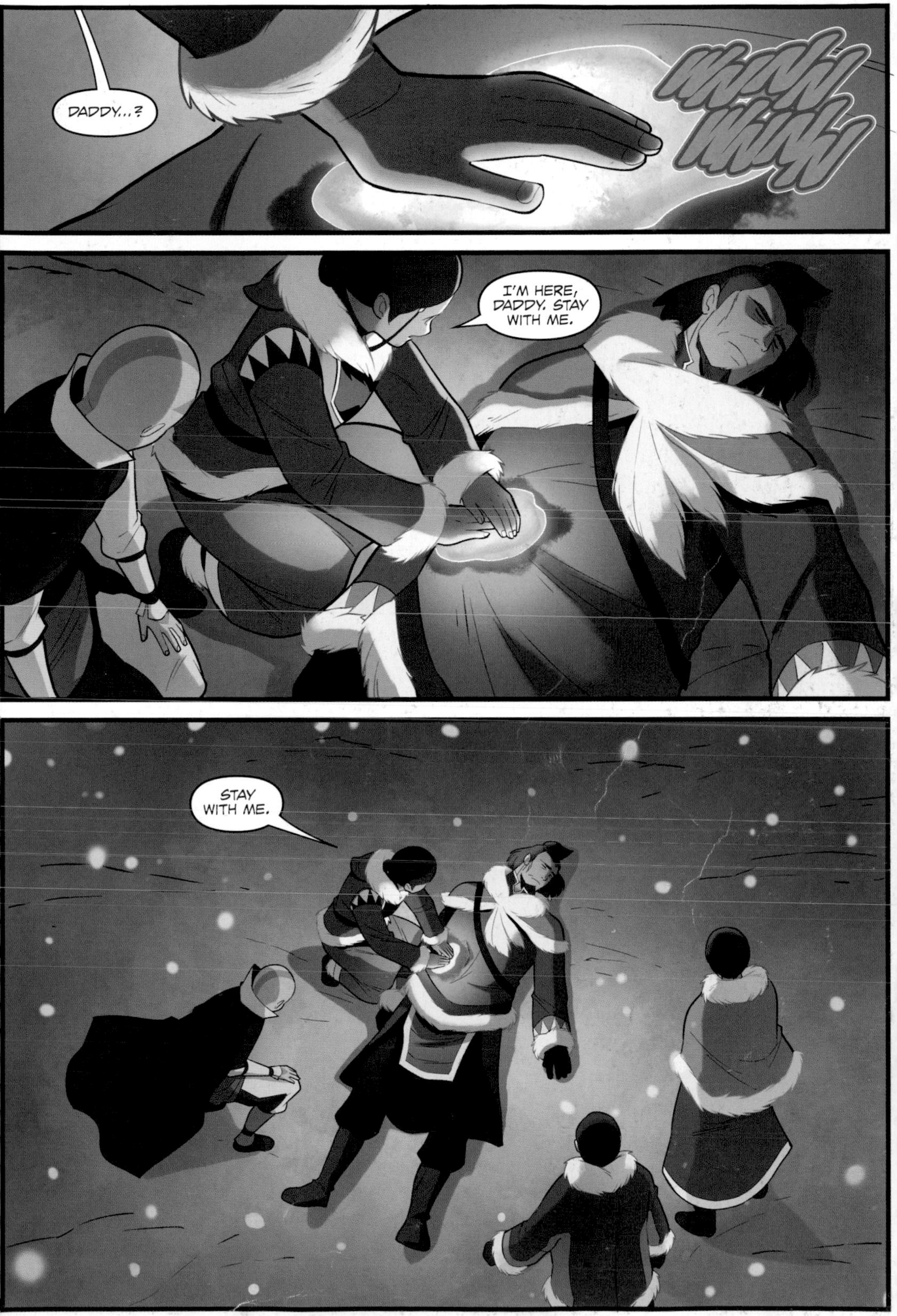
DADDY...?
I'M HERE, DADDY. STAY WITH ME.
STAY WITH ME.

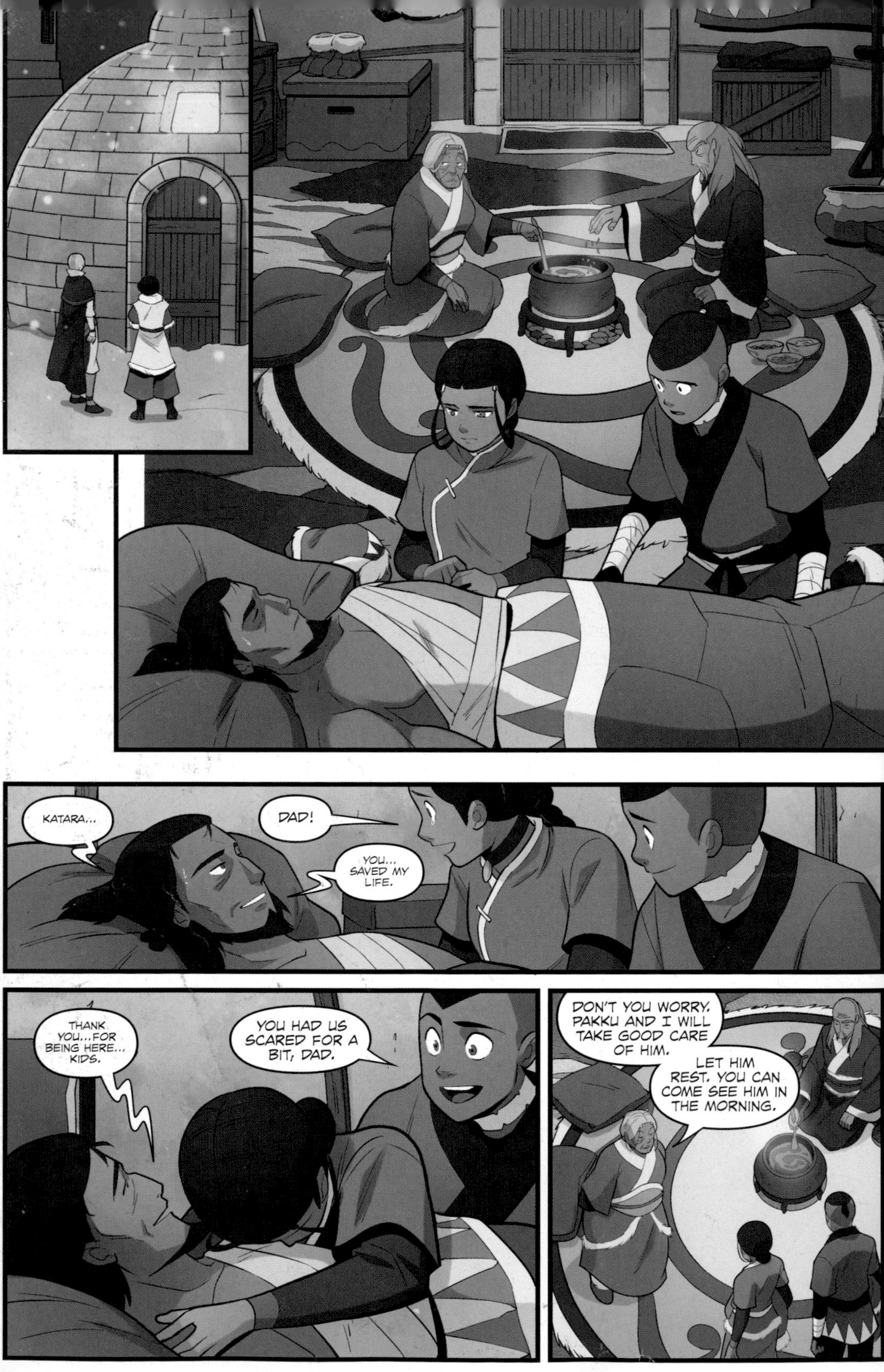
KATARA...
DAD!
YOU... SAVED MY LIFE.
THANK YOU...FOR BEING HERE... KIDS.
YOU HAD US SCARED FOR A BIT, DAD.
DON'T YOU WORRY. PAKKU AND I WILL TAKE GOOD CARE OF HIM.
LET HIM REST. YOU CAN COME SEE HIM IN THE MORNING.

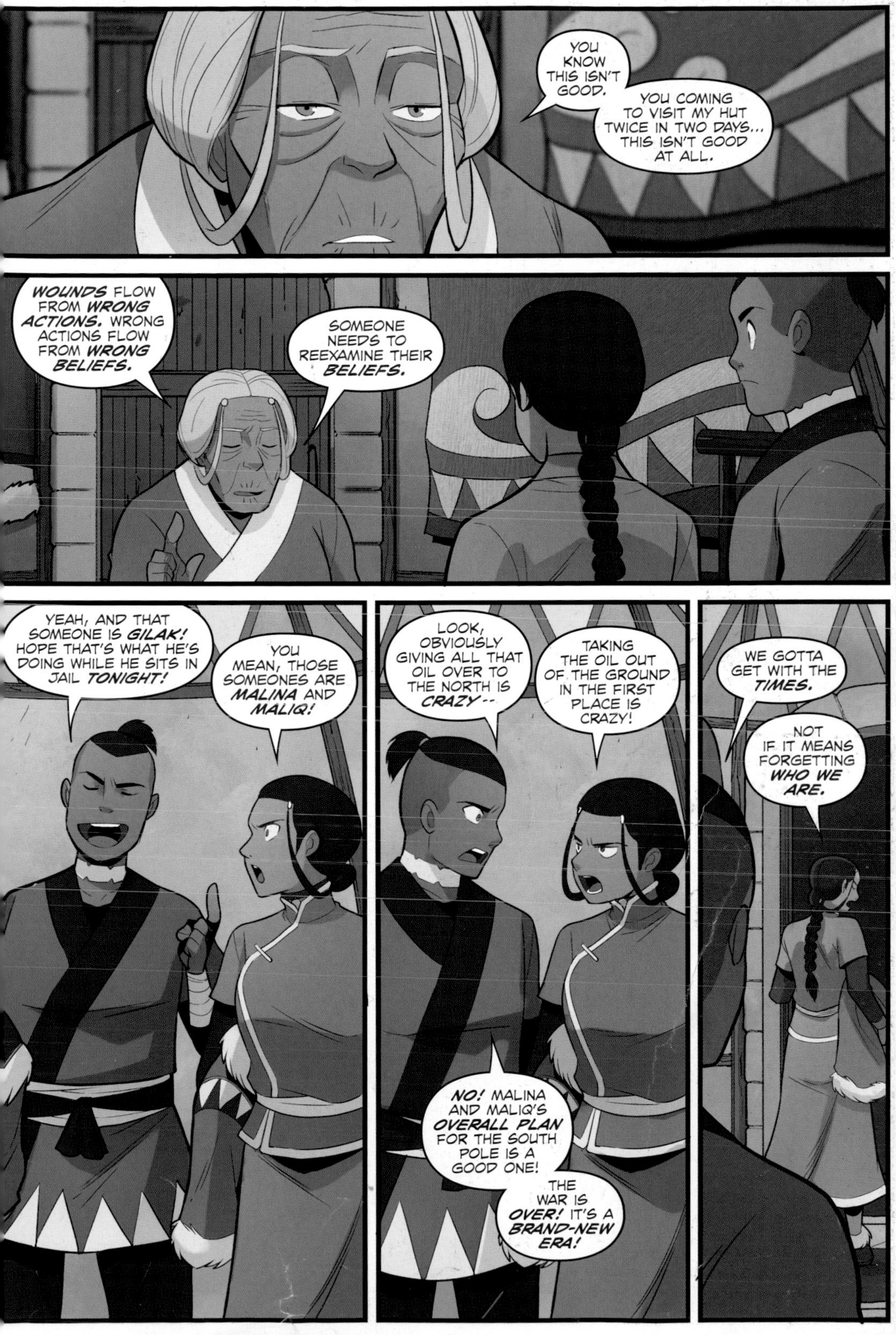
YOU KNOW THIS ISN'T GOOD.
YOU COMING TO VISIT MY HUT TWICE IN TWO DAYS... THIS ISN'T GOOD AT ALL.
WOUNDS FLOW FROM WRONG ACTIONS. WRONG ACTIONS FLOW FROM WRONG BELIEFS.
SOMEONE NEEDS TO REEXAMINE THEIR BELIEFS.
YEAH, AND THAT SOMEONE IS GILAK! HOPE THAT'S WHAT HE'S DOING WHILE HE SITS IN JAIL TONIGHT!
YOU MEAN, THOSE SOMEONES ARE MALINA AND MALIQ!
LOOK, OBVIOUSLY GIVING ALL THAT OIL OVER TO THE NORTH IS CRAZY--
TAKING THE OIL OUT OF THE GROUND IN THE FIRST PLACE IS CRAZY!
NO! MALINA AND MALIQ'S OVERALL PLAN FOR THE SOUTH POLE IS A GOOD ONE!
THE WAR IS OVER! IT'S A BRAND-NEW ERA!
WE GOTTA GET WITH THE TIMES.
NOT IF IT MEANS FORGETTING WHO WE ARE.

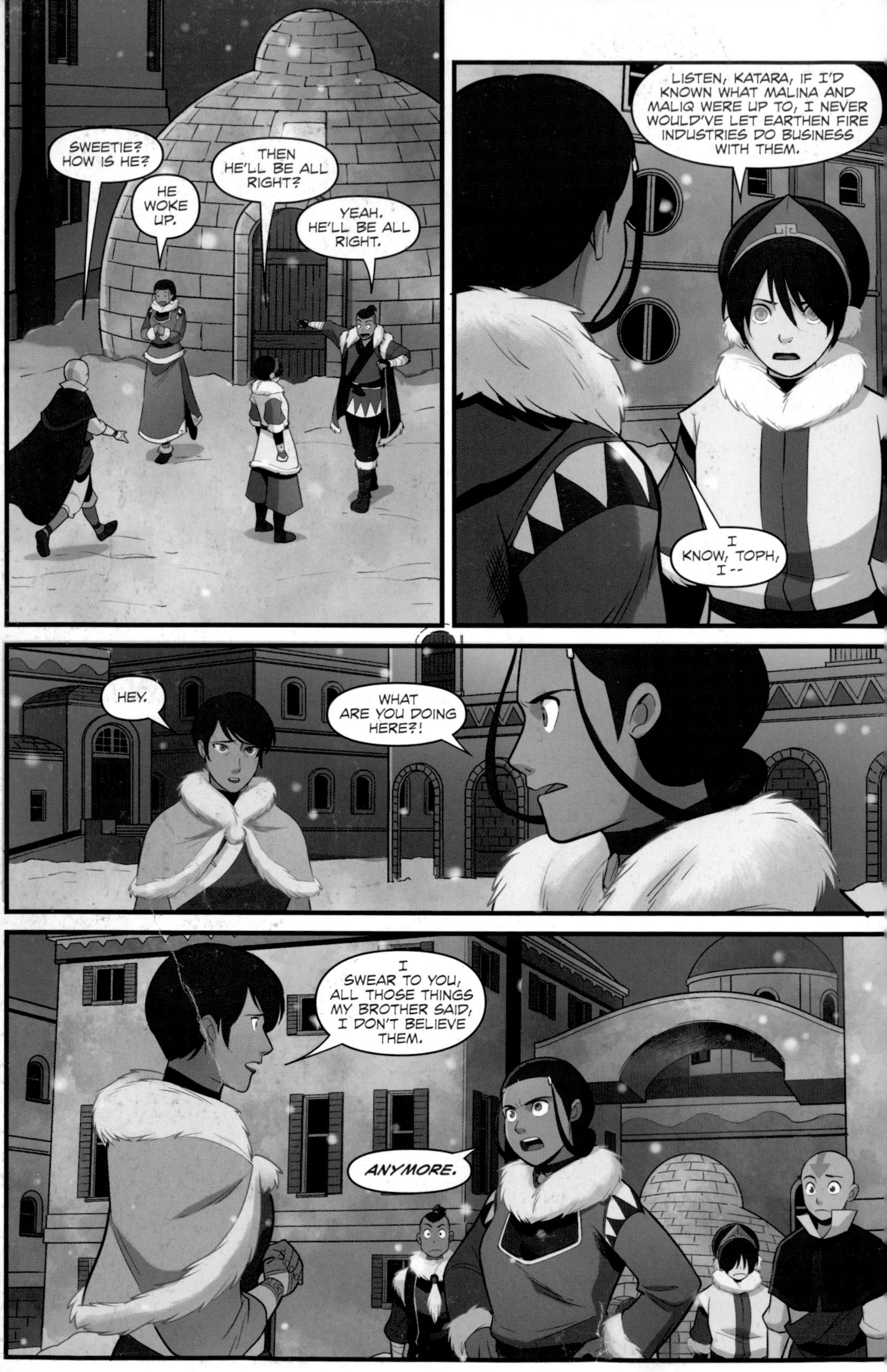
SWEETIE? HOW IS HE?
HE WOKE UP.
THEN HE'LL BE ALL RIGHT?
YEAH. HE'LL BE ALL RIGHT.
LISTEN, KATARA, IF I'D KNOWN WHAT MALINA AND MALIQ WERE UP TO, I NEVER WOULD'VE LET EARTHEN FIRE INDUSTRIES DO BUSINESS WITH THEM.
I KNOW, TOPH, I --
HEY.
WHAT ARE YOU DOING HERE?!
I SWEAR TO YOU, ALL THOSE THINGS MY BROTHER SAID, I DON'T BELIEVE THEM.
ANYMORE.

WHAT DO YOU MEAN?

YOU DON'T BELIEVE THEM *ANYMORE,* NOT AFTER YOU *"FELL IN LOVE"* WITH MY DAD.

BUT WHAT HAPPENS WHEN YOU FALL *OUT* OF LOVE, MALINA?

KATARA, IT GOES DEEPER THAN THAT.

I'M GOING TO ASK YOU AGAIN -- WHAT ARE YOU DOING HERE?!

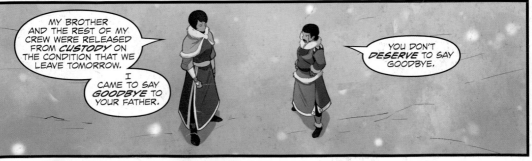

MY BROTHER AND THE REST OF MY CREW WERE RELEASED FROM *CUSTODY* ON THE CONDITION THAT WE LEAVE TOMORROW.

I CAME TO SAY *GOODBYE* TO YOUR FATHER.

YOU DON'T *DESERVE* TO SAY GOODBYE.

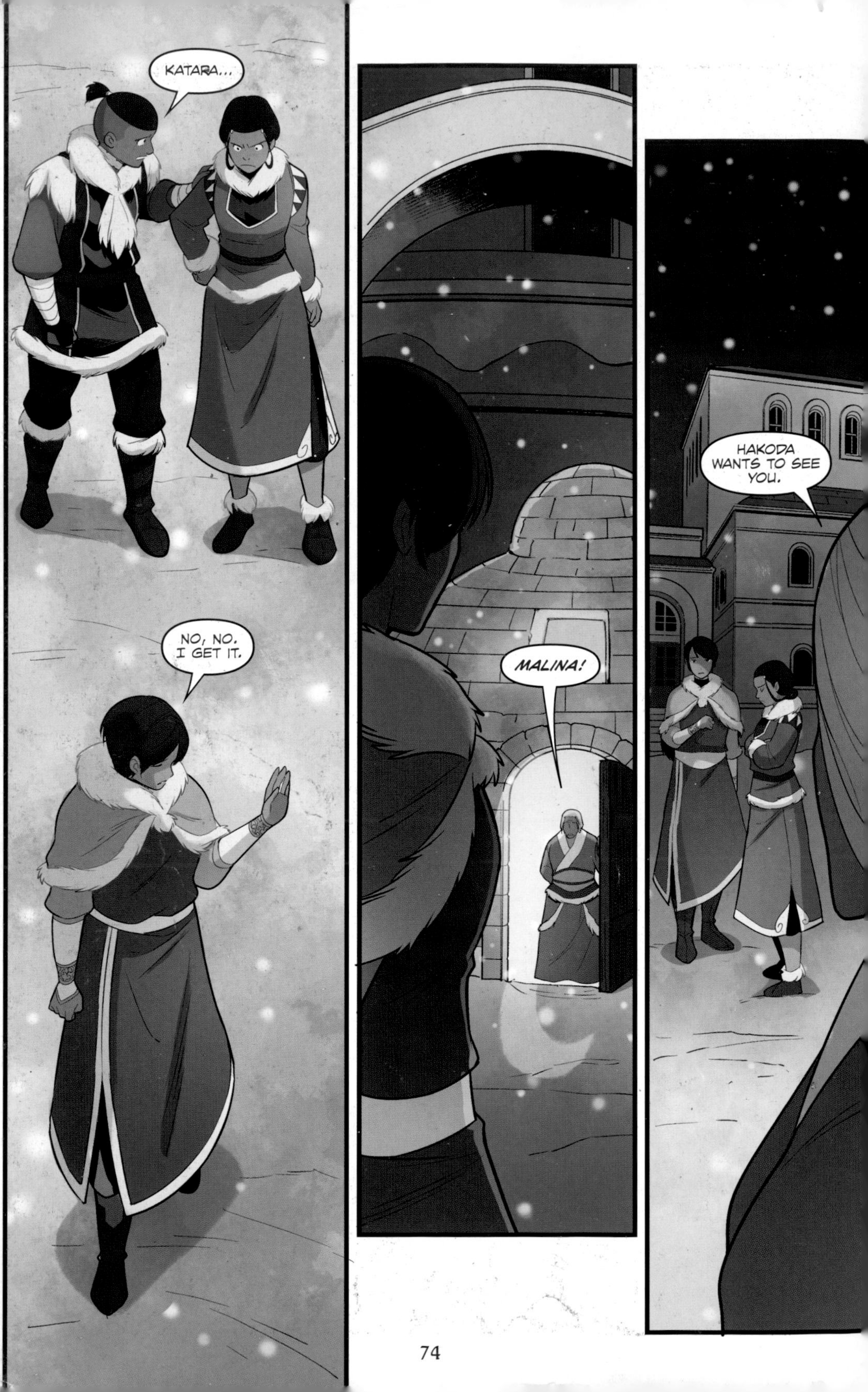
KATARA...
NO, NO. I GET IT.
MALINA!
HAKODA WANTS TO SEE YOU.

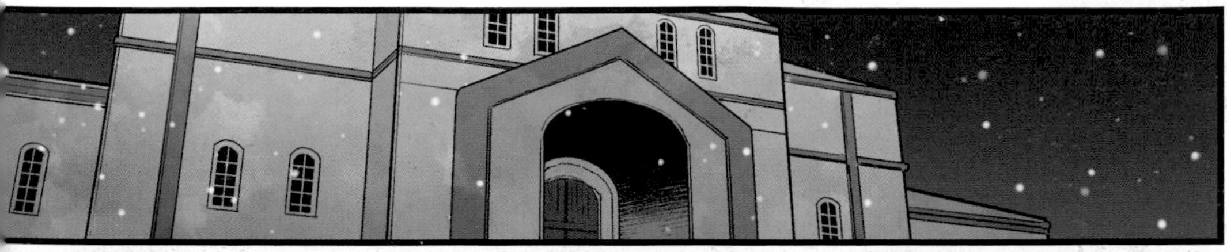

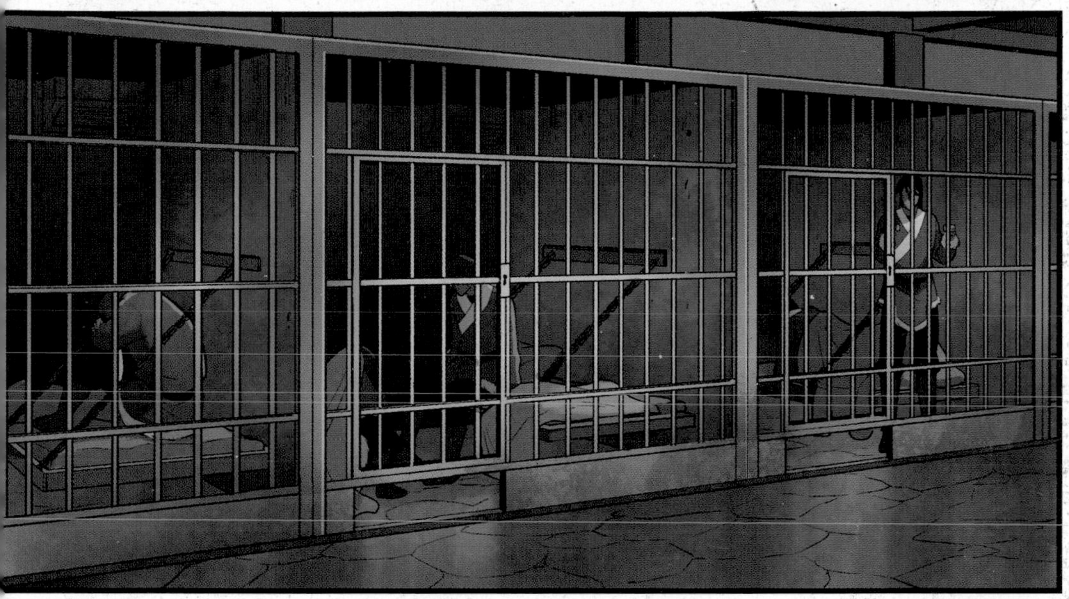

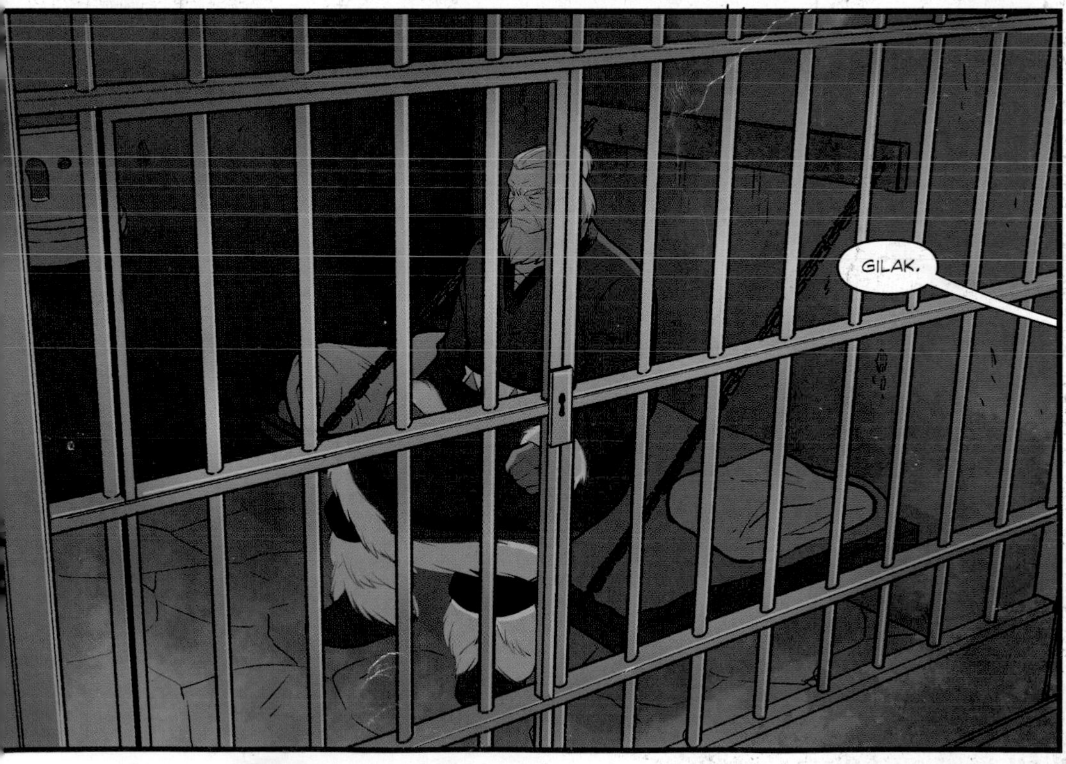
GILAK.

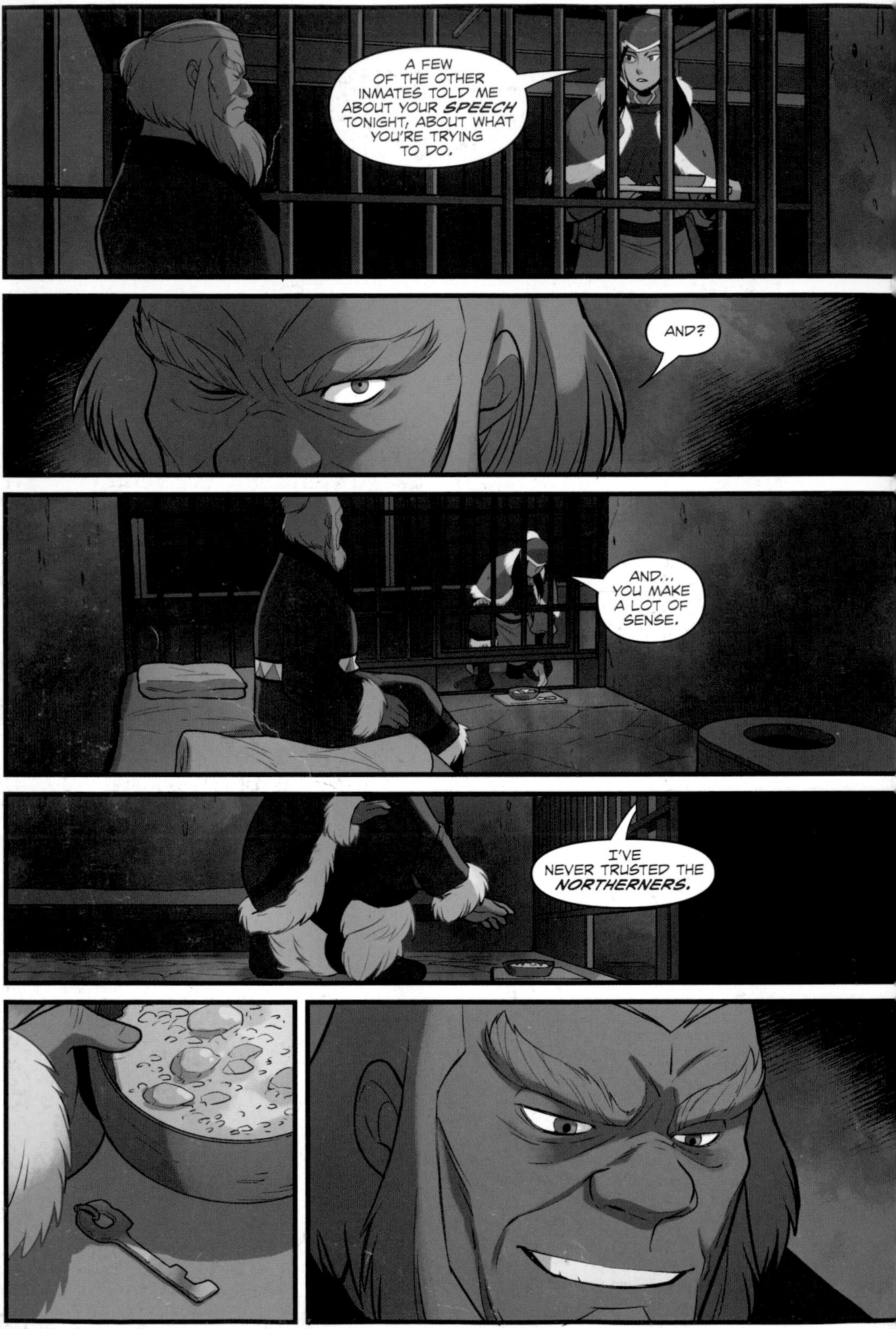
A FEW OF THE OTHER INMATES TOLD ME ABOUT YOUR *SPEECH* TONIGHT, ABOUT WHAT YOU'RE TRYING TO DO.
AND?
AND... YOU MAKE A LOT OF SENSE.
I'VE NEVER TRUSTED THE *NORTHERNERS.*

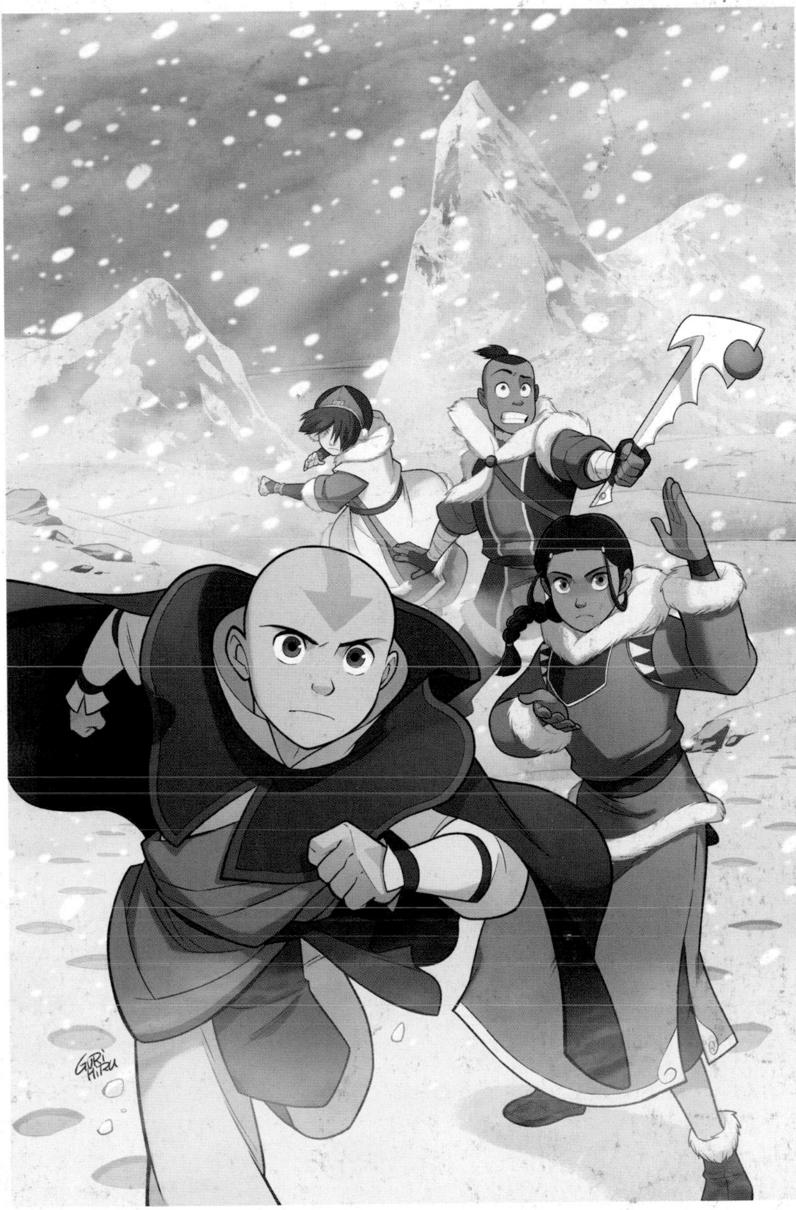
GURI HIRU

COMING IN APRIL 2017

The fate of the Southern Water Tribe is revealed in . . .

NORTH AND SOUTH · PART THREE

AVATAR
THE LAST AIRBENDER

BE PART OF THE INCREDIBLE JOURNEY!
Check out the best-selling graphic novels by acclaimed writer Gene Luen Yang.

Avatar: The Last Airbender—The Promise Library Edition
978-1-61655-074-5 $39.99

Avatar: The Last Airbender—The Promise Part 1
978-1-59582-811-8 $10.99

Avatar: The Last Airbender—The Promise Part 2
978-1-59582-875-0 $10.99

Avatar: The Last Airbender—The Promise Part 3
978-1-59582-941-2 $10.99

Avatar: The Last Airbender—The Search Library Edition
978-1-61655-226-8 $39.99

Avatar: The Last Airbender—The Search Part 1
978-1-61655-054-7 $10.99

Avatar: The Last Airbender—The Search Part 2
978-1-61655-190-2 $10.99

Avatar: The Last Airbender—The Search Part 3
978-1-61655-184-1 $10.99

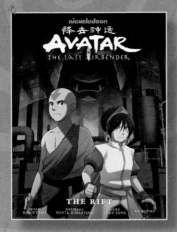

nickelodeon
降世神通
AVATAR
THE LAST AIRBENDER
THE RIFT
BRYAN KONIETZKO
MICHAEL DANTE DiMARTINO
GENE LUEN YANG
GURIHIRU

Avatar: The Last Airbender—The Rift Library Edition
978-1-61655-550-4 $39.99

Avatar: The Last Airbender—The Rift Part 1
978-1-61655-295-4 $10.99

Avatar: The Last Airbender—The Rift Part 2
978-1-61655-296-1 $10.99

Avatar: The Last Airbender—The Rift Part 3
978-1-61655-297-8 $10.99

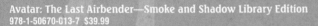

nickelodeon
降世神通
AVATAR
THE LAST AIRBENDER
SMOKE AND SHADOW

Avatar: The Last Airbender—Smoke and Shadow Library Edition
978-1-50670-013-7 $39.99

Avatar: The Last Airbender—Smoke and Shadow Part 1
978-1-61655-761-4 $10.99

Avatar: The Last Airbender—Smoke and Shadow Part 2
978-1-61655-790-4 $10.99

Avatar: The Last Airbender—Smoke and Shadow Part 3
978-1-61655-838-3 $10.99

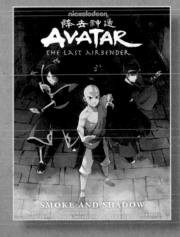

Avatar: The Last Airbender—
North and South Part 1
978-1-50670-022-9 $10.99

Avatar: The Last Airbender—
North and South Part 2
978-1-50670-129-5 $10.99

Avatar: The Last Airbender—The Art of the Animated Series
978-1-59582-504-9 $34.99

Avatar: The Last Airbender—The Lost Adventures
978-1-59582-748-7 $14.99

AVAILABLE AT YOUR LOCAL COMICS SHOP OR BOOKSTORE.
To find a comics shop in your area, call 1-888-266-4226
For more information or to order direct, visit DarkHorse.com or call 1-800-862-0052

DARK HORSE BOOKS

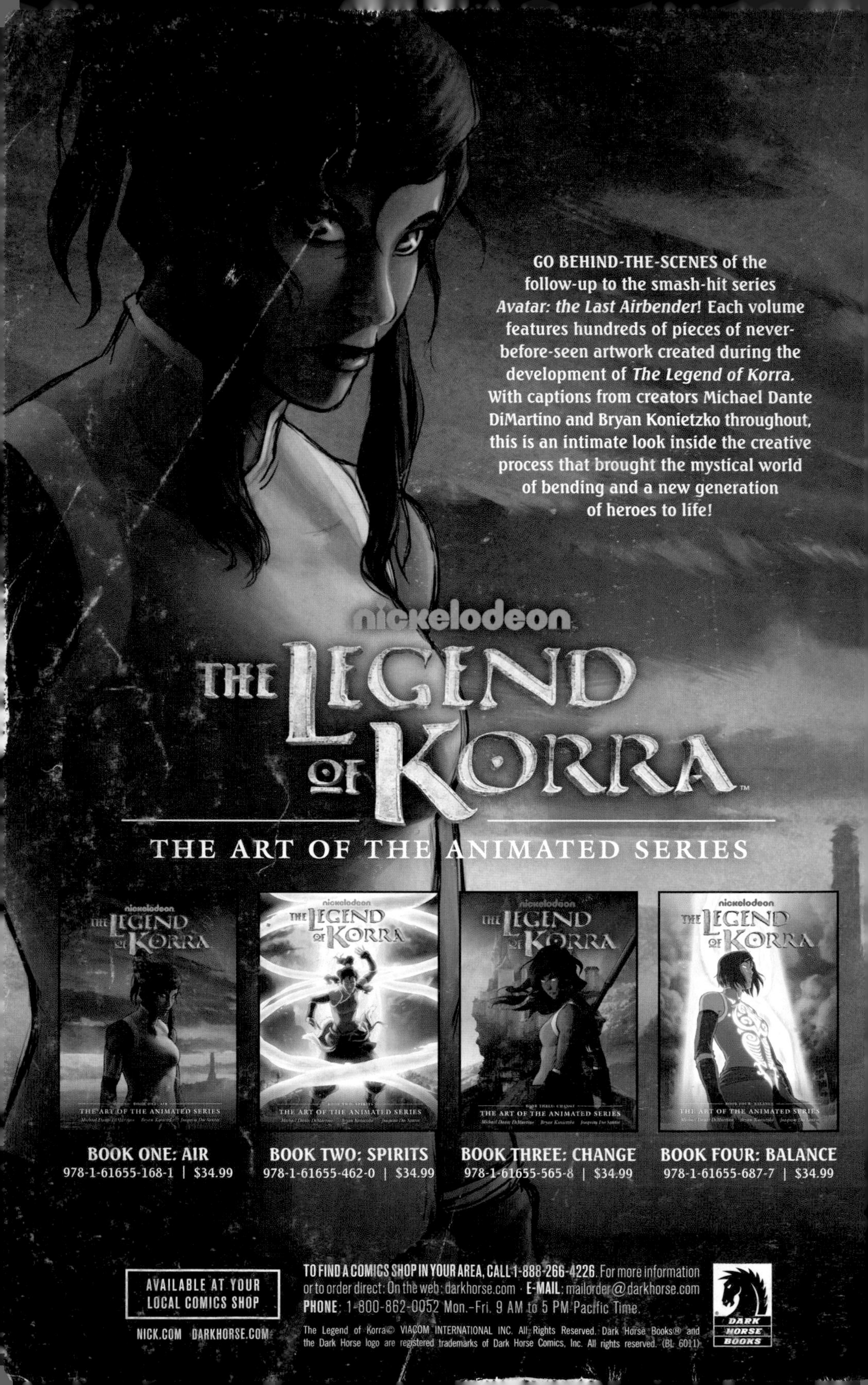
GO BEHIND-THE-SCENES of the follow-up to the smash-hit series *Avatar: the Last Airbender*! Each volume features hundreds of pieces of never-before-seen artwork created during the development of *The Legend of Korra*. With captions from creators Michael Dante DiMartino and Bryan Konietzko throughout, this is an intimate look inside the creative process that brought the mystical world of bending and a new generation of heroes to life!
nickelodeon
THE LEGEND OF KORRA™
THE ART OF THE ANIMATED SERIES
BOOK ONE: AIR
978-1-61655-168-1 | $34.99
BOOK TWO: SPIRITS
978-1-61655-462-0 | $34.99
BOOK THREE: CHANGE
978-1-61655-565-8 | $34.99
BOOK FOUR: BALANCE
978-1-61655-687-7 | $34.99
AVAILABLE AT YOUR LOCAL COMICS SHOP
NICK.COM DARKHORSE.COM
TO FIND A COMICS SHOP IN YOUR AREA, CALL 1-888-266-4226. For more information or to order direct: On the web: darkhorse.com · E-MAIL: mailorder@darkhorse.com
PHONE: 1-800-862-0052 Mon.–Fri. 9 AM to 5 PM Pacific Time.
The Legend of Korra© VIACOM INTERNATIONAL INC. All Rights Reserved. Dark Horse Books® and the Dark Horse logo are registered trademarks of Dark Horse Comics, Inc. All rights reserved. (BL 6011)
DARK HORSE BOOKS